AFRICAN AMERICAN PASTORAL CARE
REVISED EDITION

AFRICAN AMERICAN PASTORAL CARE

REVISED EDITION

EDWARD P. WIMBERLY

Abingdon Press

Nashville

AFRICAN AMERICAN PASTORAL CARE
REVISED EDITION

Library of Congress Cataloging-in-Publication Data

Wimberly, Edward P., 1943–
   African American pastoral care / Edward P. Wimberly. -- Rev. ed.
     p. cm.
   Includes bibliographical references.
   ISBN 978-0-687-64949-5 (binding: pbk., adhesive perfect : alk. paper)
   1. Pastoral care. 2. African Americans--Religion. I. Title.

   BV4011.3.W495 2008
   253.089'96073--dc22

                                      2008011896

08 09 10 11 12 13 14 15 16 17—10 9 8 7 6 5 4 3 2 1

MANUFACTURED IN THE UNITED STATES OF AMERICA

CONTENTS

119416

PREFACE TO REVISED EDITION

The challenge of revising a book that was originally published in 1979 is daunting. The difficulty of such a task emerged first when I was asked to revise *Pastoral Care in the Black Church*, originally published in 1979. The result was *African American Pastoral Care*, which appeared in 1991 but was so substantially different from the 1979 volume that it was given a new name and marketed as completely new. Nonetheless, the 1991 publication began as a revised edition.

What made *African American Pastoral Care* different from the 1979 book was the emphasis on the role of the African American pastor as storyteller. In the role of storyteller, the African American pastor was to respond to the emotional, interpersonal, and spiritual needs of persons in crises, drawing on the rich indigenous cultural legacy of storytelling within the African American community. Robert Dykstra coined this the indigenous storytelling tradition.[1] *Pastoral Care in the Black Church*, however, focused more on the mobilizing role of the African American pastor, which was to draw on the rich support systems of corporate pastoral care in its sustaining and guiding functions. The second publication kept the sustaining and guiding emphases, but they were envisioned as an extension of the indigenous storytelling model.

What distinguishes this third edition from the original 1979 and 1991 editions is an awareness that the world we live in as African Americans is vastly different from the world we lived in fifteen to twenty-seven years ago. The 1979 and 1991 editions were written with the assumption that the relational and culturally connected African American community was intact. In fact, the indigenous storytelling model assumed that the connected relational village existed and that the faith worldview was undergirded by a *soul theology* with many interrelated and interconnecting themes.[2] Thus, when the storyteller told stories, he or she was drawing on a genre of material that the vast majority of African Americans, whether Christians or not, would understand. Such a worldview, however, can no longer be assumed.

Several key figures in the African American community help us recognize that the village that used to characterize the African American community has collapsed. Homer Ashby in *Our Home Is Over Jordan* chronicles the loss of the village and how we need to recapture the village functions that once sustained African Americans.[3] He points out that fragmentation and relational disconnections among African American people are fueling the violence, crime, and confusion rampant in our community.

Cornel West also recognizes that nihilism has overtaken the African American community, and attention to the loss of community is essential for us to thrive. For him, nihilism is not a philosophical theory but a relational reality involving the loss of love and communal connections, the loss of purpose, and the loss of meaning.[4] The point that West makes is that those relational traditions that in the past enabled African Americans to thrive despite racism have all almost collapsed, and something drastic must take place to reverse the trends.

Accompanying the loss of village connections and the increasing presence of nihilism in the African American community are certain key themes that must be addressed by African American pastoral care in the twenty-first century.

The first theme is that racism and classism characteristics of the past have not disappeared. They are still real, but the structural forms that gave racism and classism their power are no longer needed. Racism and classism still have political and economic structural components, but they have a life of their own that transcends these structures and lies deep in the psychic lives of all persons living within the United States. For example, we recently completed the midterm elections where the Democratic Party retook the United States Senate and the House of Representatives. The subsequent discussion on *Good Morning America* on November 15, 2006, was whether racism and sexism were deeply rooted in the unconscious of all Americans. The discussion was whether unconscious racism and sexism would prevent either Hillary Clinton or Barack Obama from becoming President of the United States. This was further fueled by a concern that unconscious racial and gender realities could prevent an African American or a woman from being President. The most "positive" sign about the *Good Morning America* show was that the participants realized that race and gender biases are so deeply rooted in our psyches that they are intractable realities that will never disappear; they will just change form. This realism is healthy in that it keeps us from being disappointed when these realities surface and hit us in the face. Racism, classism, and sexism are active realities with which all must continually struggle. These realities are cosmic in nature, as the biblical Letter to the Ephesians says, "For our struggle is not against enemies of blood and flesh, but against the rulers, against the authorities, against the cosmic powers of this present darkness, against the spiritual forces of evil in the heavenly places" (Ephesians 6:12).

Racism is real, but the collapse of the village has made African Americans more vulnerable to racism and being recruited into negative identities than in the past. In the past, the village provided the relationships necessary to transcend the meanness of racism, but such buffers are becoming extinct. Relational connections not only helped provide meaning and worth to our lives, but they also prevented us from being recruited into the dominant culture's racial attitudes and prejudices.

Despite the reality of the collapsing village, this revised edition will continue to focus on the reality that the indigenous storyteller is still essential for the black church in the twenty-first century. Robert Dykstra points out that newly formed contemporary images and metaphors for ministry help us diagnose and heal the traumas of our age and social location. He suggests that the indigenous storyteller of the African American faith tradition provides the image or metaphor that brings constructive engagement for dealing with contemporary problems facing African Americans.[5]

Indeed, the metaphor "indigenous storyteller" still remains powerful for giving guidance to constructive approaches for recreating village functions in contemporary black churches. Though we are in the winds of losing the village connections that have sustained us, the storytelling tradition remains viable. Telling and retelling stories evokes creative imaginations for reestablishing village functions that must continue to sustain us and help us strive to be resilient despite horrendous problems that we face.

We cannot underestimate the evocative, powerful nature of the role of the storyteller in black churches. In the first edition, *African American Pastoral Care* demonstrated that the role of storyteller was to proclaim the eschatological presence of God's reign. It went on to say that how God's reign announced God's eschatological plot of salvation continues to unfold in our lives, our communities, and our world. The storyteller tells the stories of God's eschatological presence in our lives, while the stories themselves draw us into God's eschatological plot. Being drawn into God's unfolding plot of salvation brings meaning, hope, purpose, and perspective to our lives. The plot also stimulates our creative imaginations about how we can construct better lives for ourselves and our communities.

The most significant aspect of storytelling is that it triggers within individuals, marriages, families, extended families, and villages unconscious memories that provide imaginative resources for reconstructing our villages. The values that undergirded our collective lives in the past have not disappeared. Rather, they have gone underground into our collective unconscious psyche, where they are waiting to be released and utilized for rebuilding our village connections and functions. Telling and retelling stories from the Bible, from our faith communities, and from our everyday lives as people of faith evokes concrete images and memories that propel us into imaginatively recreating our village connections.

As we proceed in updating and revising this new edition, our focus will be on lifting up the role of storytelling. It will stress that storytellers can evoke unconscious stories that can be resources for our present and future in order to re-village our community. Moreover, this book will stress the role of storytelling in addressing the concerns that will occupy African American churches in the near future as well as in linking our churches with emerging emphases. This book will critique the post-modern concerns of defining human worth and value in commodified and marketing terms; understand the political nature of pastoral care, particularly when it comes to editing the negative stories into which we have been recruited; link our efforts with government initiatives to address promoting African American fatherhood and healthy marriage and family; and address concerns centered around human sexuality, including the AIDS pandemic. This new edition will introduce how Scripture functions in the healing, sustaining, and guiding aspects of pastoral care in black churches.

Finally, this new edition will draw on the concept of eschatological practice as a pivotal and seminal concept for explicating the village functioning of indigenous storytelling and listening. Practice is a contemporary metaphor for grasping how certain cultural traditions are established and reestablished in communities. For example, practice is rooted in activities that are based on norms that are established by certain professions that are legitimated or sanctioned by authorities who are given the rights and privileges to carry out these activities. Sanctioned practice is rooted and grounded in criteria of competence and knowledge. It is legally defined, providing permission to carry out certain functions.[6] Eschatological indigenous African American storytelling practice, however, by its very nature emerges from within a context outside of the mainstream of sanctioned, legalized, and validated authoritative practice. In fact, the eschatological indigenous African American storytelling tradition emerged out of unsanctioned and unauthorized established practices, and its origin was in the need to fashion a set of meaning-making practices that enabled African Americans to survive in a culture that denied us the right to define our own value and worth as human beings. Thus, eschatological indigenous African American storytelling is an artistic and imaginative practice of meaning-making that, although derived from necessity, focused on God's presence. What grief and sorrow African Americans experienced in the present was, in all actuality, was being ameliorated or improved by God's glorious, unfolding future.

To understand the eschatological indigenous African American storytelling tradition, it is critical to understand how slavery forced African Americans to fashion a system of practice outside and beyond the watchful eye of the master, drawing on biblical stories and their own experiences with slavery. What early African Americans took away from their encounters with God and biblical stories in the midst of slavery was being grasped by the eschatological plot of God drawing them into God's future, which was manifesting itself on a daily basis. They witnessed God creating a new world that was present but not yet. They encountered what the Gospel stories were telling about the coming of a new age called the kingdom of God. Consequently, through their own creative encounters with God, they created an imaginative set of practices known as indigenous storytelling that form a master narrative or eschatological plot "best exemplified in the stories of the exodus of the Hebrew children from Egypt and of the resurrection of Jesus from the dead."[7]

Indeed, indigenous African American eschatological storytelling emerged as an imaginative encounter with God in the midst of slavery and has become a continuing source of caring up to the present time. This same creative and imaginative practice is essential in the contemporary African American church and community given the nature of the collapsing village. Essential to the task of recreating village functions within African American churches and communities is a new phenomenon that some are calling the Bible as Pastor Movement.[8] Part of this movement is an effort to reclaim the power of Scripture to shape the caring ministry of the church and to redefine the nature of biblical authority.

Biblical authority presents some interpretive difficulties, especially relating to violence. In the effort to redefine the nature of biblical authority, there are two approaches to deal with texts of terror that can lend themselves to the abuse of women and avocation of war. According to Rod Hunter, one approach is the progressive nineteenth-century notion of progressive revelation through Scripture where troublesome passages were rejected in favor of a pure gospel. The second approach is to recognize that troublesome passages are thrown into the midst of redemptive passages. This second approach sees the Bible as ambiguous and dangerous.[9] There is a third alternative, however, and this third alternative is the eschatological plot orientation growing out of African American Christians' encounter with God in the text.

What African Americans take away from the encounter with God in Scripture is the eschatological plot, understood as redemptive and liberating. Thus, African Americans interpreted the texts of terror within the context of God's unfolding drama of salvation, and the eschatological plot had to be envisioned in light of the coming of God's rule on earth. For example, in the lives of African Americans, slavery, racism, and oppression are real, but within the eschatological plot of God, they are not the final chapters. There is more to come. The texts of terror are episodes in the unfolding story of God, but they are not the final outcome. God is working out of God's purposes; and the texts of terror, like the chapters of slavery, oppression, and racism, will be overcome.

Thus, the theme the "Bible as Pastor" will be value-added in this new edition. In fact, it is out of this understanding of the Bible as Pastor that the indigenous storytelling model first emerged. More precisely, the indigenous model of storytelling emerged from African Americans encountering God in the text and finding themselves included in God's salvation drama where they felt themselves cared for, valued, and included in God's future. It is this inclusion in the unfolding drama of the coming of God's reign on earth and African American Christians' participation in it that motivate and empower the indigenous storytelling model.

Edward P. Wimberly, Ph.D.
Atlanta, Georgia, June 2007

CHAPTER ONE

A NARRATIVE APPROACH TO PASTORAL CARE

Since the publication of *Pastoral Care in the Black Church* in 1979, I have become firmly convinced that black pastors approach pastoral care through narrative. It is this insight about such an approach to ministry that motivated me to write a supplement to that book.

A truly narrative style of pastoral care in the black church draws upon personal stories from the pastor's life, stories from the practice of ministry, and stories from the Bible. Genuine pastoral care from a narrative perspective involves the use of stories by pastors in ways that help persons and families visualize how and where God is at work in their lives and thereby receive healing and wholeness.

This method of pastoral care involves several dangers. The primary danger is that the pastor's own life experience is so subjective and personal that it might be used imperialistically to lead some pastors to think that "my way is the only way." Second, the narrative approach might lead some to think that a personal indigenous style is all that is needed and that formal training has no place. Third, the narrative style might cause the pastor to be less empathetic and thereby transform counselee/parishioner-centered counseling sessions into pastor-focused counseling sessions.

However, a narrative approach need not be imperialistic, nonempathetic, or pastor-focused. Storytelling can facilitate growth and empathy, be parishioner-centered, and contribute to the essential qualities of any caring relationship. For example, this approach can enable the pastor to enter the parishioner's world of experience and see things through the parishioner's own eyes. It can help the parishioner take full responsibility for making his or her own decisions. It can enable the parishioner to be specific when describing events. This approach can also help the counselor openly discuss things that are occurring between the counselor and the parishioner. Finally, it can help the counselor express his or her feelings about what is taking place in the parishioner's life in ways that lead to growth.

This book is an attempt to demonstrate that an indigenous approach to caring that relies upon storytelling is one style of pastoral care and counseling that takes place in the black church. Not only is this style already used by pastors, it is a basic method used by black people, both lay and clergy, to care for one another. Therefore, this book is written for clergy, seminary students, and laypeople who are interested in knowing how they have cared for one another and how they can improve that care.

THE NATURE OF STORYTELLING

Black pastors use many types of stories—long stories, anecdotes, short sayings, metaphors—to respond to the needs of their parishioners. Most specific instances in life situations lend themselves to story formation. For example, stories can be used to address the normal crises people face daily, such as birth, a child's first day at school or at day care; transitions from childhood to adolescence or from adolescence to adulthood; and mid-life, old-age, and death transitions. Likewise, story formation can occur during periods of crisis: losses such as illness, accidents, changes in residence, and a variety of other events that pose threats to someone' s emotional or physical well-being. Stories also can be developed during selective phases of counseling to facilitate the counseling process.

In all these ways, stories function in the caring setting to bring heal-ing and wholeness to the lives of persons and families within the black pastoral care context. Henry Mitchell and Nicholas Lewter call such sto-ries *soul theology*, the core belief system that gives shape to the world, that shows how African American people have come to grips with the world in a meaningful way.[1] Narratives and stories embody these core beliefs that permeate the church life of African Americans, and black pastors and congregations draw on this narrative reservoir when caring for their mem-bers. These narratives suggest ways to motivate people to action, help them see themselves in a new light, help them recognize new resources, enable them to channel behavior in constructive ways, sustain them in crises, bring healing and reconciliation in relationships, heal the scars of memo-ries, and provide guidance when direction is needed.

Soul theology makes up the faith story that undergirds the stories used by black pastors and parishioners in caring for others. And how that faith story has brought healing and wholeness through storytelling to the lives of African American people is the subject of this book.

THE FAITH STORY

Mitchell and Lewter point out that crisis situations spontaneously ex-press core beliefs.[2] Core beliefs are deep metaphors, images that point to the plots or directions of life. These core beliefs, rooted in stories, manifest them-selves in human behavior as people attempt to live their lives. For the African American Christian, deep metaphors are related to the life, death, and res-urrection of Jesus Christ, who liberates the oppressed and cares for the down-trodden. These deep metaphors are especially informed by the Exodus story and God's involvement with God's people. These deep metaphors and core beliefs are anchored in the story of God's relationship with God's people, as recorded in Scripture and as lived out within African American churches.

The plot that gives structure to the deep metaphors of the Christian story is important to the faith story. Plots tell us why we live on earth; they point to the direction life is taking.[3] Plot in the Christian faith story shows us how our lives are connected to God's unfolding story. The faith story, therefore, answers the question of the "ultimate why" of our existence.

The dominant plot that gives life meaning for the African American Christian is what I call an eschatological plot, one that envisions hope in the midst of suffering and oppression, because God is working out God's purposes in life on behalf of persons. The eschatological plot takes suffering and oppression very seriously without minimizing their influence in life. Yet despite the prevalence of suffering and oppression, God's story of hope and liberation is unfolding. Although the final chapter of the story of liberation awaits consummation at the end of time, during many moments along life's journey, there is evidence of God's presence, bringing healing, wholeness, and liberation.

Mitchell and Lewter refer to this eschatological plot that underlies the faith story of black Christians as the providence of God:

> The most essential and inclusive of these affirmations of Black core beliefs is called the Providence of God in Western terms. Many Blacks may not have so precise a word for it, and they may not even know that the idea they cling to so naturally is called a doctrine. But in Africa and Afro-America, the most reassured and trusted word about our life here on earth is that God is in charge. This faith guarantees that everyone's life is worth living. The passage that expresses it best is Paul's famous word to the Romans: "And we know that God works in everything for the good of those who love him and are called according to his plan."[4]

The eschatological plot calls the Christian to faith because each must participate in life and in God's unfolding story, knowing that things will work out in the end. The eschatological plot is important because it does not minimize suffering and oppression, nor does it give suffering and oppression the last word.

A goal of the narrative approach to pastoral care in the black church has been to link persons in need to the unfolding of God's story in the midst of life. The African American pastor has narrated, and continues to narrate, stories that help people catch a glimpse of hope in the midst of suffering. It is by identifying with the story that Christians have linked themselves to purposeful directions in life, despite suffering and pain.

The eschatological plot, through which God is working out healing, wholeness, and liberation on behalf of others, has four major functions: *unfolding, linking, thickening,* and *twisting.*[5] God's plot *unfolds* one scene and one chapter at a time, and one cannot know the end of the story until the entire drama is completed. However, by identifying with faith stories, particularly stories in the Bible, one can learn to participate in God's drama, while trusting God's authorship of the drama and God's plan for the final outcome. In counseling within the black church, this often has meant that the pastor must ensure that the counselee who is identifying with a biblical story reads the whole story before coming to any conclusions. For example, it is important that one continues the story of Joseph and the coat of many colors until Joseph is occupying an important government position for the second time. To stop reading this story before its end may leave the reader feeling that life is tragic. Only at the end of the story can we see God's purposes for Joseph revealed. When one reads the entire story, one can envision hope in the midst of tragedy.

When one identifies with stories that have an eschatological plot in Scripture, one is not only pointed toward God's unfolding story in the midst of life, one is *linked* with the dynamic that informs the plot. God's unfolding story is more than a good story with which to identify. It is an ongoing, unfolding story, even today, so when black Christians have identified with that story, they also have linked their lives with the dynamic force behind the events of life. When people are linked to God's unfolding story, their own lives become different. Significant changes take place. People find that life has direction for them, that they have value as human beings. The slaves' identification with Israel's Exodus is illustrative of such positive outcomes. By linking their lives with the unfolding plot of Israel's Exodus, the slaves focused their attention on God, who was also working on their behalf to liberate them.

The eschatological plot also thickens. *Thickening* refers to those events that intrude into God's unfolding story and seek to change the direction of that story for the ill of all involved. The plot often can thicken when suffering stakes its claim on us. This thickening could be the intrusion of oppression and victimization that, for a time, hinder our growth and development; and it is at such times that we wonder whether God really cares. However, unfortunate negative interruptions are only temporary, and the story again begins to unfold in ways that help us envision God at work, seeking to *twist* the story back to God's original intention, despite the thickening that hindered the plot.

A pastor who understands the working of God through drama can link people with the unfolding of God's story. Such a pastor seeks to help parishioners develop *story language* and *story discernment* in order to visualize how God's drama is unfolding in their lives. This means that telling and listening to stories become central to the caring process. It also means that people learn to follow the plots of stories, to visualize how God is seeking to engage them in the drama as it affects their lives.

The eschatological plot, with its emphasis on God's healing presence in life despite suffering and pain, has been the driving force behind the narrative approach of the black church. By telling and listening to stories, black preachers and congregants have sought to help people envision God's work in the midst of suffering. They have sought to link people with this activity, so that their lives can have significant meaning, despite the reality of suffering.

In addition to the unfolding, linking, thickening, and twisting of plots, faith stories have four types of therapeutic functions: healing, sustaining, guiding, and reconciling.[6] These are the traditional functions of pastoral care and are very much a part of the narrative approach. However, since a narrative approach to pastoral care cannot determine the impact of a story, one cannot predetermine the impact a story might have on a parishioner or counselee. Nevertheless, stories do influence people's lives in characteristic ways: they can heal or bind up wounds caused by disease, infection, and invasion; they can sustain persons in the face of overwhelming odds and lessen the impact of suffering; they can provide guidance to those affected by the personal and interpersonal obstacles that can hinder people's ability to grow. The goal of pastoral care and counseling, from a narrative perspective, is to use storytelling to strengthen people's personal and interpersonal growth so that they can respond to God's salvation drama as it unfolds and as it has an impact on their lives.

From a narrative perspective, pastoral care can be defined as bringing all the resources of the faith story into the context of caring relationships, to bear upon the lives of people as they face life struggles that are personal, interpersonal, and emotional. The gospel must respond to the personal needs of individuals and families as they face life struggles. This is best done in the private context of pastoral care, rather than in the public context of preaching or worship. Because the context and intent of preaching, worship, and pastoral care are different, the use of storytelling in each ministry is also different.

STORY-LISTENING

So far, this discussion has been devoted to the storytelling aspect of caring. One might conclude that the telling of stories is the main dimension of a narrative approach to pastoral care. The danger of overemphasizing storytelling, however, is that it may ignore the needs of the person facing life struggles. Story-listening is also an important dimension of African American pastoral care, and the narrative approach is a story-listening as well as a storytelling approach.

Story-listening involves empathically hearing the story of the person involved in life struggles. Being able to communicate that the person in need is cared for and understood is a result of attending to the story of the person as he or she talks. *Empathy* means that we attend to the person with our presence, body posture, and nonverbal responses. It also means using verbal responses to communicate that we have understood and are seeking to understand the person's story as it is unfolding. The caregiver also gives attention to and acknowledges the significant feelings of the person as they are expressed in the telling of the story. It is only when the story has been fully expressed and the caregiver has attended to it with empathy that the foundation is laid for the utilization of storytelling.

The emphasis must be on story-listening to avoid the trap of shifting the focus away from the needs of the person facing life struggles. There are two important ways to prevent this potential abuse of storytelling. First, a growing body of literature on storytelling within the context of counseling and psychotherapy can assist pastors in knowing how to use their own life stories in helpful ways. Second, pastors need to grow in their own personal life so that their life stories and participation in the faith story will be a reservoir of conflict-free and anxiety-free stories. The ways one can use new resources from the counseling literature and can grow so that one's life will be an anxiety-free source of stories will be addressed in later chapters.

STORYTELLING AND RETELLING THE STORY

In an age where the village connections are being continually lost, it is important to utilize communal means of storytelling and story-listening as a vehicle for reconstructing village functions. Michael White put forward one such village reconstructive narrative method, the definitional ceremony. In the year 2000, I attended the Milton H. Erickson Institute in Anaheim, California. Here my narrative understanding expanded by leaps and bounds. Michael White, an Australian family therapist, presented a video of a group of Aborigines whose lives had been disrupted by technological advances. Their traditions for dealing with loss and grief had been disrupted, and he was asked to help them come together in order to grieve the loss of a family member who had been murdered. He called his approach to them the definitional ceremony. The definitional ceremony is a narrative process of storytelling and retelling the story where a person who has an emotional concern or issue tells his or her story. It is then followed by a group of persons retelling the original storyteller's story in light of what struck those hearing the story when the original storyteller told the story.[7] The original storyteller becomes part of the audience, and those who were part of the original audience become storytellers and retell the story they heard, drawing on their own lives. Following the retelling of the story, the original storyteller becomes the storyteller again and begins to retell the story in light of what he or she heard from those who retold the original story. The end result of this phase of retelling the story is that the original storyteller gets an opportunity for catharsis by expressing strong feelings as well as by deriving new perspectives on what he or she had been experiencing. The original storyteller also feels cared for and loved by those who took the time to listen and retell the story. A support system of relational ties is thus created, which sustains the person as he or she goes through the grief process. Thus, the supportive and maintaining function of the village was re-created through the telling and retelling of stories.

An example of this process of telling and retelling stories will be re-created based on a number of telling and retelling story sessions in which I have participated. This particular story is about the grief and loss resulting from sexual abuse triggered by the death of a parent who was the sexual abuser.

The setting was a class in Inner Healing that I have taught since 1985. In the Inner Healing class, the focus is on the student's own life issues, and the goal is to create an atmosphere where students feel comfortable to tell stories with which they feel comfortable. One way to create an atmosphere of openness where students feel free to share their own stories is for the professor to begin the process of storytelling himself or herself. Thus, depending on the topic, I would share some concerns out of my own life that I felt comfortable sharing. I do not customarily share stories with which I am currently struggling, however. Rather, I share stories out of my own life with which I have dealt in the past and about which I might feel comfortable sharing more information if asked. The major point of telling my own story is not only to demonstrate transparency but also to make sure that the story is such that it will trigger students to think about their own stories rather than focus on my story. If the stories that I tell are unresolved and recent, they might stimulate interest in my own story rather than enable others to tell their own stories.

Before getting into the actual process of telling and retelling stories, it is important to envisage the classroom as a laboratory for re-creating village functions. Every class in seminary is an opportunity for the formation of a village. Here the concept of village refers to the process of becoming a support system of relational ties that fosters an environment for enabling members of the class to maintain their emotional, interpersonal, and spiritual integrity in the face of life's complexities.

Indigo was a member of the Inner Healing class. The topic was domestic violence and how domestic violence serves as a relational means of recruiting family members into negative identities for the purpose of building up the perpetrator of the violence at the expense of the victim. The process of recruiting through the use of domestic violence involves getting the potential victim to internalize a negative identity so that the victim becomes a willing participant in his or her own self-destruction and is always available for abuse by the victimizer. As the topic of domestic violence unfolded late in the semester, Indigo felt comfortable in bringing up her own story of domestic violence that was clearly on her mind due to the death of her biological father.

The background to Indigo's story was that she had been in seminary for one year. The first semester went well, but in the second semester a series of deaths began to take place in her family. It began with the death of her grandmother's boyfriend who had sexually molested her when she was a young girl. She was raised by her grandmother, and her grandmother's boyfriend routinely sexually molested her while her grandmother was at work. He was supposed to be watching her after school. He would tell her not to tell anyone what he was doing, threatening more harm to her. Thus, she kept the experiences of sexual abuse quiet, fearing reprisals.

His death brought up memories of her past abuse at his hands that she had not shared with others. She pointed out that his death propelled her into the process of remembering key incidences from the past that she knew she had to tell. She felt all right about recalling the memories of the past abuse, but then a series of tragic events began to take place that she did not understand. These events piled on top of the death of her abusing boyfriend of her grandmother, and these events made her feel that she was under attack for no reason. Her daughter suffered a miscarriage, and she had to take off time from school to take care of her. Her older brother suddenly fell ill and died. She was very close to this brother, so the loss really devastated her. Finally, a favorite grandaunt died, and this almost overwhelmed her. She felt that she had to tell her story for fear that she was going to fall apart.

After hearing her story, I attempted to communicate a few empathic statements, picking up on the fact that she seemed to not understand why all of this was happening to her at this time. She indicated assent to this interpretation. I asked her if she felt all right if I asked others in the class to retell her story and retell it based on the insights that occurred to them as they heard her story. I told her she would get a chance to respond to their retelling of the story after we heard from the others. She agreed to the process.

One person retold the story she heard by focusing on the abuse that she had sustained at the hand of a family member. She indicated that it had come at a very vulnerable time in her life, and she had been threatened with harm if she told. She also said she had carried around the pain in her life until she was an adult, and she finally had to share her story with family members because she found out that her nieces were being sexually molested in similar ways. This reteller of the story told how she exposed the secret of her own molestation when she found out about her nieces' abuse, and she said it caused a negative stir in the family. She pointed out, however, that her telling of the story eventually forced the family to face the deadly secret that was having a negative impact on the lives of others. She said the cycle of abuse was finally disrupted, and the perpetrator was dealt with in the family.

Others came forward and told of their own abuse. One student told of how seminary caused her to face the fact that her father had sexually molested her. She said she went home and confronted her father and her mother as a result of her experiences in seminary. She said her father, to her surprise, confessed to his sexually molesting her, and he indicated he would do whatever she needed to become whole again. He agreed to enter into his own therapy, and he paid for her therapy. She indicated that she was still in the process of healing, and that she felt good about bringing the molestation out in the open.

Several other stories were told. One last story that was told addressed the reason these events took place all at once. This reteller of the story said that she had undergone many losses when she entered seminary. She said she could not figure it out until one day someone mentioned to her that she was under a demonic attack. She pointed out she did not want to accept that answer since it was not part of any theology that she had ever considered. She changed her mind, however, when she realized that the series of negative events began to happen to her when she made a decision to go to seminary. She said when she realized that she was under attack from Satan, she drew closer to God in her prayer life. After a period of time in prayer and after deciding to not give up seminary and to continue toward ordination, she felt better and the attacks stopped.

Following the retelling of Indigo's original story, she got a chance to retell her own story. She told of how supported she felt, and how important it was for her to realize she was not alone and isolated in her story. She said the idea of being under a satanic attack made sense, and she was going to make it a point to address it in her prayer life. She also indicated that she had shared the story of her sexual molestation, and other family members who had been sexually abused by this same step-grandparent came forward and sought her out. She said the retelling of the stories gave her courage to continue on in seminary and to continue to be a healing presence in her family.

Following the telling and retelling of the original story, I had one of the women in the class say a closing prayer. The following week I began to talk about the significance of the definitional ceremony as a means of sustaining and healing persons as well as a means of recapturing the village functions of reinforcing relational ties that sustain people in integrity in the midst of crises and stress.

THE SIGNIFICANCE OF THE NARRATIVE APPROACH

Significance refers to assessing what has been said in light of the role of the narrative approach in re-creating the re-villaging effort in black churches, the effort to evoke and mine the unconscious re-villaging sources lying dormant in the lives of African Americans through eschatological practices, and how the Bible is a vehicle driving this process. The concept of re-villaging rests in a notion that "the village is that small communal network of persons linked together by a common biological, family, cultural heritage living in a particular geographical location where frequent interaction is a reality."[8] Moreover, the village performs certain functions. For example:

> Symbolic functions refer to the ways in which narrative, metaphors and images comprising the worldview and spiritual perspectives of village life work to bring meaning to its members. Ritualistic functions refer to those repetitive patterns of communal life that reinforce the village worldview and values and that assist persons' movement through life transitions. Maintenance functions refer to those support systems practices and values that help people maintain themselves holistically when encountering the problems of life. Reparative functions are those healing endeavors in which the community engages after someone has been hurt or broken. Mediating functions are those mechanisms that transmit the worldview and spiritual values from one generation to the next.[9]

The key is that the definitional ceremony provides a context for carrying out the village functions. According to Michael White, settings for storytelling in a fragmented village are hard to find and they must be created. The definitional ceremony provides such a venue.[10]

THE LIMITATIONS OF THE NARRATIVE APPROACH

In addition to the danger that a narrative approach might focus on the pastor's needs rather than those of the parishioner or counselee, other limitations to the narrative approach must be addressed as well. First, the storytelling approach is not designed to be the only approach to the problems people face. There are times when direct and confrontational approaches are more appropriate. Sometimes pastors in the priestly role must help people face the truth and assess whether the story the person is living out is healthy or unhealthy. The key is that the pastor must help people judge their own stories in light of the faith story. When there is some discrepancy between the person's own story and the unfolding faith story, this truth should be pointed out by the pastor. Moreover, the pastor should help the counselee align his or her own life story with God's unfolding story.

Another limitation of the storytelling method is that it may assume that the people in need have Bible knowledge. But what about those who are unchurched or have very few roots in the institutional church? Although the storytelling approach does presuppose some familiarity with biblical stories, many such stories can be used to address the problems people present, if careful thought is given to the reason the stories are being told. One cannot assume that people will find Bible stories objectionable or irrelevant to their needs simply because of their lack of familiarity. Nor can one assume that there is no religious interest on the part of some counselees. However, this does not give the pastoral counselor license to tell religious stories without prior thought or permission from the counselee. It is always appropriate to ask for permission prior to telling the story. And one need not confine oneself to religious stories. There is rich material in African American folklore from which to draw as well.

SUMMARY

Black pastors, to care for persons through storytelling,

1. Draw upon their own experiences in life and ministry, as well as upon Bible stories.
2. Use storytelling in the context of caring relationships, to foster personal, interpersonal, and emotional growth.
3. Use stories as a means of enriching people's awareness of God's drama unfolding in their lives, despite suffering.
4. Link persons with the unfolding of God's drama in ways that bring healing, sustaining, guidance, and reconciliation.
5. Enable parishioners to develop a language that helps them discern God's work in their lives.
6. Use the resources of the church and the narratives that undergird them to attend to the needs of individuals, families, and small groups. This includes worship and ritual.
7. Use stories in the art of counseling to make points, suggest solutions, facilitate cooperation, increase self-awareness, and discover resources for counseling.
8. Use conflict-free and anxiety-free narratives to help people grow emotionally and interpersonally.

CHAPTER TWO

PASTORAL CARE
AND WORSHIP

CARING AND ADDICTION

The role of the local congregation in pastoral care can best be discerned in the worship life of the black church, but it is not only in corporate worship in the large congregation that pastoral care takes place. Pastoral care in worship also takes place in small groups gathered for Bible reading, exhortation, and prayer and song services to heal physical ills, emotional wounds, and relational hurts. Such services include small groups of people who care about the well-being of others.

Although black church worship has been celebrated in literature as emotionally therapeutic for African American Christians, the strength of the worship life has not been limited to the Sunday morning service. As in many vital churches, small group meetings called to minister to specific needs of persons and families also have been strong within black churches. In Wednesday night prayer and Bible study meetings, significant hurts have been healed. In the pastor's study, many small groups have prayed for and with people in difficulties. When the choir has surrounded its members in need, significant caring has taken place.

AFRICAN AMERICAN PASTORAL CARE

These small group settings are often informal, but ritual is present nonetheless. Here ritual is referred to as repetitive actions that have as their goal the drawing of people into the major story of the faith community. Whenever the goal of ritual draws persons into the major story of the faith community, worship takes place. Moreover, when ritual and worship draw persons into the major story of the faith community, worship and communal resources are brought to bear on personal needs; and when the emotional, interpersonal, and psychological needs of persons are met in the context of ritual and worship, pastoral care takes place.

This chapter looks closely at the role of the laity as caretakers within a ritual and worship context. The emphasis is on defining the role of the laity as caretakers, along with the pastor, in a ritual and worship context. The primary focus is on small groups, from three to forty-five people, called together to perform special rituals of pastoral care for persons in need. Attention also is given to helping the laity define or understand their caring role within the ritual life of the church.

Key to this chapter are the concepts of indigenous storytelling as evoking eschatological practice, or developing public means of creating new and innovative means of evoking the eschatological plot in the lives of the congregation.

A THEOLOGY OF MINISTRY

In assisting the laity in its role within the caring ministry of the church, it is important to look at the total ministry of the church. Only when the total ministry is understood is it possible to visualize the role of the laity in pastoral care within the ritual and worship context.

Caring within a local black congregation is a response pattern to God's unfolding story in its midst. This unfolding story is one of liberation as well as healing, sustaining, guiding, and reconciling. As a response to God's story, the caring resources of the local black church are used to draw those within the church, as well as those outside the church, into God's unfolding story. By being drawn into God's story, people find resources of care and love to meet their everyday needs. As a response to being drawn into God's story and finding care and love, pastors and laity alike commit themselves to be part of God's ongoing story of liberation and healing. Being committed to God's unfolding story means not only drawing others into that story, but helping others envision the working of God's story in the midst of their own lives.

Caring is a ministry of the church and cannot be understood apart from the ecclesiology or theology of the church. The mission of the church, from a narrative perspective in the black church, is the continuation of God's story. It is the story of liberation and healing as understood centrally in the book of Exodus, as continued through the life, death, and resurrection of Jesus Christ, and as revealed today within local churches empowered by the Holy Spirit. The unfolding story of God's rule and reign is characterized by God's ongoing activity to bring all dimensions of the world under God's leadership and story for the purposes of liberation, healing, and wholeness. This results in personal and social transformation.

The purpose of God's rule is to draw all people and nations into God's story. God's story is a story of the defeat of the powers of evil, oppression, and suffering. It is a story of healing and wholeness when people live meaningful lives in community. God seeks to draw people and communities into this story so that the resources of God's reign can be made available to them for their growth and development. Thus, God's rule and reign is about drawing people into God's story so that they might be shaped by the story and begin to see reality the way it is shaped by God's hand and teachings.

The mission of the church in drawing others into the story of God has implications for (1) the church in worship; (2) the church as a caring community; (3) the church in care and nurture; and (4) the church in service.

19

First, God's unfolding story shapes worship. Worship is the act of people in the local church as they gather to celebrate and give praise to God for being drawn into God's story. It is celebration of the fact that they have found meaning and purpose in their lives as a result of being drawn into the story. However, worship is more than an act of celebration and praise; it is a time when the people of God are drawn deeper into the unfolding story of God and are further shaped by this movement. Their vision and character are transformed because of this increased participation in God's story. Their attitudes, behaviors, intentions, and dispositions take on more of the character of God's story. In other words, increased involvement in God's story leads to an increased ability to be concerned about the things that God is concerned about within the church and within the world.

Second, the total life of the local church is shaped in light of God's unfolding story. The local church, as a community, shapes the individual stories of its members into a communal story that reflects the unfolding story of God. This communal story is shaped by the vision that is caught when the community interacts as the people participate in God's unfolding story. As God is revealed in the unfolding drama, the church as a community can glimpse God's intention for it and for the world. The individual stories of all the people are thus shaped by the vision revealed in God's continued action in their midst.

Third, care and nurture result from faithfulness to God's vision revealed within the community. Care given to another because God cares for us draws people into the richness of God's caring resources for healing, sustaining, guiding, and reconciling. Caring is visualizing God's story as it unfolds in churchgoers' lives—in spite of the suffering, pain, and crises—and then helping people respond to God's presence and story in their lives. Nurture in the context of care is an awareness of what it means to be a caregiver in God's unfolding story within the life of the church. Nurturing takes seriously the importance of understanding persons in need, as well as understanding the best way to respond to them, particularly within a ritual context.

Caring and nurturing are part of the mission of God's church as that mission unfolds concretely within the church. As such, pastoral care draws people into God's story of healing, sustaining, guiding, and reconciling. It also helps God's people care for others by helping others see themselves the way God sees them, see God at work in their lives, and know how to respond to God's caring presence. All this takes place in the context of caring relationships.

Finally, community outreach is also a response to being drawn into God's story. While the larger community may not share the same faith story, the church plays a role in assuring that the resources needed for positive mental health and wholeness are available to the community. Sometimes this means that the local church provides the mental health services that are needed. At other times, the church may ensure that a community agency provides the mental health programs needed in the community. In these ways, the local congregation begins to engage in community organization and political activity, working toward the goal of emotional and mental health and wholeness.

A Case Study of Caring through Ritual

Over the years, when I have referrals from pastors for counseling services, I make an attempt to keep the pastor informed of the progress of the counseling. When possible and when the need arises, I may also draw the pastor into the counseling to help achieve a certain goal. Of course, this is done with the permission of those in counseling and is based on sound counseling principles. On some occasions, I may also involve carefully chosen relatives or friends from the church to achieve therapeutic ends. This also must be carefully thought out and planned by the pastoral counselor with the counselee.

One such occasion, when I sought not only the participation of the pastor but also the help of key people within the life of the church, concerned the case of a woman whose husband was using cocaine. I present this case as an example of one means through which both pastors and laity may be involved in pastoral care and counseling.

This case illustrates how ritual and worship can be utilized for thera-peutic ends in very small groups of caring persons. The aim is to enable the reader to draw from this case some general insights that pastors can employ to continue the therapeutic function of worship in the black church.

Often pastors, as well as pastoral counselors, are approached about the drug use of family members. This is often very difficult to approach, espe-cially when the user is not open to receiving the help needed. The fol-lowing case is an example of one model of help, called "intervention." In this model, loved ones and a professional confront the user with the ne-cessity of getting help. The intervention shows the user that the family cares about him or her and, at the same time, indicates that they want something done about the problem.

This case is one in which a couple was referred to me for marital coun-seling by a pastor who was aware of the husband's drug use. The pastor felt limited in his resources for dealing with the problem and sought my help. As the problem emerged, it became clear to me that the situation was so serious that the husband needed to be hospitalized for the treatment of co-caine addiction. It was at this point that I began to work with the couple toward the goal of hospitalizing the husband.

Initially, the husband described himself as an occasional weekend user and claimed that he had not been using it much lately. At first his wife seemed unconcerned about the problem; later she would realize that she had been what the literature calls a "codependent," a person who con-tributes to the addiction by making excuses for the addicted persons, bail-ing them out of trouble, covering for their embarrassing moments, and refusing to confront them with the way their behavior has hurt the code-pendent. Codependents often find it very difficult to allow their loved ones to suffer the consequences of their actions.

When the husband missed the third session after calling me that morn-ing to indicate he would be present, I began to realize that something very serious was taking place. He also missed the fourth session, but he attended the fifth session by himself. At that time he disclosed that the problem was more serious and that he was losing control over cocaine. During the following weekend, the wife called me to indicate that she was at her wit's end and that something had to be done. She was ready to try anything because she could not go on the way things were.

During the sixth session, the husbamd indicated that he was a serious user of cocaine and that he was freebasing.[1] On some days, his habit cost $400. He had just lost another job and had begun to sell things, including his wedding ring. He knew that his life would completely deteriorate unless he stopped. At age fifty, he saw his life heading for serious ruin.

He found it hard to understand why he did what he did. He wanted to act differently but felt he did not have the power. He remembered the time when he did not smoke, drink, or take drugs, and he began to explore the feeling he had had since childhood that he was oppressed by Satan. He did not believe he was possessed, but he remembered thinking as a child that he had once met Satan face-to-face. When he had told his mother, she had laughed, saying that he must have looked in the mirror. He felt his life was doomed to failure.

A breakthrough came when we were discussing how his wife had bailed him out of trouble. When she had given him money to buy back his wedding ring, he got the ring, but spent some of the money on cocaine. Deeply hurt, his wife indicated to him that she realized she needed to let him go and that she would stop bailing him out of trouble.

He responded quickly by protesting, "You can't leave a person at a time when they are wounded the most. You can't abandon me to this problem." When I asked him if he could explain what he meant, he said that prayer was the only thing that could help him. He talked about a time when a small group of people prayed for his nephew, who had been an alcoholic. Since that prayer, his nephew had been dry and recovering. His wife then informed him that the nephew was part of the Twelve-Step program of Alcoholics Anonymous and had been working with other alcoholics ever since he started to recover. I began to explore with both of them the possibility of arranging a similar kind of small group prayer meeting. He liked this idea, and we began to plan the time when we would come together for a ritual of prayer for his cocaine addiction.

The first thing we planned was the goal for the prayer meeting. We agreed that the focus would be on behalf of the husband to enter a treatment program for cocaine addiction. He didn't want to be in a white treatment program, and I was able to find one administered by African American people. He did want to do something about treatment, but he hoped that prayer would prevent him from having to go into treatment. He felt that his goal was to bind the work of Satan that was controlling the events in his life. I pointed out that although prayer was basic and foundational, he would require a period of recovery in a hospital following our ritual of healing. I indicated that prayer and treatment need to work together. His wife believed in the power of prayer, but she also knew that prayer would be the beginning of his treatment, rather than the end. He agreed to begin with the ritual of prayer and then wait to see what would happen.

Once we agreed on this goal, we discussed a possible date and the persons who would be part of this small group to pray for healing and deliverance. We decided that the pastor, the pastor's wife, the couple's goddaughter, and a recovering cocaine addict would be there with us. I left it to the couple to call the people and make the arrangements.

Finally the day arrived. When all were present, the pastor began to explore the problem with the husband. They talked back and forth, and the pastor quoted several Bible verses that focused on the availability of God's grace for times such as this. The pastor knew enough about the husband to use verses that made him think. One of the husband's major concerns was his status in life—that all his friends seemed to be making something of their lives. The pastor knew that the husband focused his life in the wrong direction for success and that his problem had spiritual roots. The pastor also shared his struggle with his own son, who had been hooked on drugs, and he seemed to have great empathy for the husband's predicament, although he knew the man needed to go into treatment for help. The husband seemed to feel cared for by the pastor.

Others offered words of encouragement, and some quoted helpful Bible verses. When the pastor asked me what I thought, I said I had listened with great joy to their dialogue, when the husband had indicated that he knew the treatment program was necessary. I had waited for the husband to indicate that himself, and I pointed out that his ultimate recovery was his embracing of the purpose he knew God had created him to fulfill. He had known for some time that his ministry would be to help others like himself. In fact, he had begun to attend school for that purpose when he first encountered cocaine. The group acknowledged that everyone knew there was a special purpose for which he was called, and all felt he had to embrace this purpose as part of his healing.

Then as we stood in a circle holding hands, the pastor asked me to begin the prayer and said that others could follow. I began by thanking God for all God's servants who were concerned enough about their loved one to join in prayer for his healing and deliverance. I indicated the reason we were here, asking God to visit us in a very special way with God's power and Spirit. At that point, the focus was on the husband and his feeling about being oppressed by Satan. I asked God to come against the evil that was befalling the husband, and as I prayed, the others responded, "In the name of Jesus." I asked that the work of Satan be bound in the name of Jesus and that the husband be empowered with the Holy Spirit to fight the difficult battle ahead. The members of this special prayer group responded, "In the name of Jesus."

After I finished, others began to pray. Concern was raised for the wife and the difficulties she has encountered. Others prayed that the husband would do what he needed to do. The godchild prayed for their future relationship and indicated how much that relationship meant to her.

When the pastor prayed, he seemed to be in direct touch with the husband's thoughts. He addressed all his arguments about not going into treatment; he addressed the needs he would have over the next few weeks in treatment. Then he prayed for the binding of Satan's work and quoted Scripture. When he prayed for the husband, he touched his head and his stomach, as if to find the bodily source of the problem. Then he read Ephesians 3:14-21, emphasizing the prayer that God strengthen the husband in the inner man, so that Christ would take up permanent residence in his heart.

Following this reading, the wife collapsed. The frustration of all the years of pain seemed to have left her weak. Her husband and the whole group began to minister to her. They prayed with her and began to hum in low voices until she felt better.

Two days after the prayer meeting, the wife told me that her husband had entered treatment. She expressed her appreciation, and we talked about the spouse program that she needed to take part in at the hospital. I indicated my desire to follow through with counseling once the program had ceased.

NARRATIVE REFLECTION

Worship was a vehicle used in pastoral care to help draw the husband into God's unfolding purposes for his life. The worship service included sharing, music, Bible quoting, and praying. The aim of that worship service was to enable the husband to see that people loved and cared for him and that God was in the midst of his life, seeking to bring wholeness to it.

In the ritual of worship, he acknowledged an awareness of God's presence and work in his life. He knew that God had a purpose for him, but he was slow to allow himself to embrace God's vision and story in his life. Those who cared for him asked God to give him the power to enter the treatment program because they knew that on the other side of treatment, there was a new story for his life.

Worship also challenged the values that were the center of his life. He had a hard time letting go of his images of success, but worship introduced him to the fact that the story he was embracing would lead him into further destruction. Therefore, worship sought to draw him out of the old story that was leading him to destruction and take him into a new story that would lead to hope and fulfillment.

Worship was also a vehicle of God's grace for the couple. The Scriptures that were shared assured the husband that he was loved and that he was a child of God. Ephesians 3:14-21 summarized our meeting together and helped summarize our intent, which was to strengthen him inwardly so that he could fully engage in the recovery process. By sharing experiences from his own life and disclosing that his own son had been crippled by drug addiction, the pastor showed his care, letting the husband know that his own scenario was the same as that of others before him and that those who loved him would not give up on him.

The most crucial dimension of the worship service was the sharing of the witness of God at work in the husband's life by those who loved the couple. He could not see it, nor could he believe that God had any interest in our prayers for him. It was important for those who cared to witness what they saw God doing, and it was this sharing and witnessing that laid the foundation for reassessing his own life story.

In summary, the small group prayer meeting was designed (1) to share with the husband God's love and grace; (2) to share with him in ways that would draw him further into God's unfolding story; (3) to give him encouragement to enter treatment; and (4) to enable him to discern his role in God's salvation drama.

THE ROLE OF THE PASTOR

The role of the pastor in caring and addiction is to create an environment of concern and care; to enable the worshipers to pray and sing, keeping the needs of people in mind; and to use Scripture and exhortation to encourage those in crisis to have the courage and strength to meet the emotional and interpersonal tasks.

The use of worship to address the early concerns of addiction is very appropriate. In the husband's case, the roots of his addiction were the feelings of being unloved and not cared for by others or by God. He used drugs and alcohol to try to stamp out the feelings of worthlessness and unlovability, but the more he tried to get away from those feelings, the more he went into bondage to his addiction. Worship and the presence of caring others spoke directly to his feelings of being unloved and worthless, and provided the basis for meeting his core needs. The pastor's role helped facilitate the mediation of grace through worship and caring relationships.

INDIGENOUS ESCHATOLOGICAL STORYTELLING TRADITION

We need to take a fresh look at this case using the concepts of indigenous storytelling and eschatological practice. While this case took place in the late 1980s and early 1990s, the loss of the village was at work, and this case provides some real material for bringing new light to our lives in the twenty-first century. The eschatological indigenous African American storytelling tradition grew out of slavery and a practice outside of the watchful eye of the master. African Americans drew on stories derived from the Bible and their own experiences with slavery. Early African Americans took away from their encounters with God and biblical stories the fact that they were being grasped by the eschatological plot of God. This plot drew them into God's future. The indigenous storyteller evoked God's story as a way to heal, but the latent product was the reinforcing of the village and its supportive community. This same tradition was at work in the late 1980s and early 1990s, and it is alive today. It was in the memory and collective unconscious of the pastor as well as those gathered together in a small healing service of worship.

Of significance was the fact that the Bible became the center of the worship intervention. The pastor chose a passage from the Letter to the Ephesians that had great significance because of the problems the church of Ephesus was having with the imprisonment of its founder, Paul. The goal of the passage chosen was for the ancient church leader to encourage those in the church of Ephesus to trust the grace that was already at work in them. The ancient writer used Paul's words to evoke courage to deal with Paul's imprisonment by calling forth what was common knowledge as a result of Paul's teaching. God's grace was at work in their inner being as expressed in chapter 3, verse 16. In fact, the writer put the words of encouragement into the form of a prayer of blessing that Jesus Christ, our Lord, would reach into his storehouse of glory to strengthen them through God's spirit in their inner person. Paul pronounces a benediction for the ability to comprehend the love of Christ and of Christ's power that was already at work in them.

The pastor drew on this biblical prayer and benediction to give not only hope and encouragement but also the power of God who was at work transforming his life. Indeed, the pastor and I were aware of the work that God was already doing in his life, and we wanted him to realize that transforming power was already working in him. Thus, the ancient tradition of eschatological practice was at work. It is this tradition that our slave parents and pastors drew on to transform the lives of slaves and ex-slaves in the steal-away worship times outside of the master's hearing and sight. The eschatological or hopeful plot that was at work was made manifest for all present, not only reinforcing the hope of the person in need but also strengthening the small village, enabling them to become a true support system. Eventually, the person recovering from addiction used the power at work in his inner being to help him edit his internalized negative story that was keeping him in bondage.

CHAPTER THREE

PASTORAL CARE
AND SUPPORT SYSTEMS

ILLNESS, BEREAVEMENT,

AND CATASTROPHIC LOSS

The crisis of loss creates a cessation and interruption of important in-
teracting patterns and sustained relationships that are taken for
granted. It is also a rupture in the existing narrative of life, because the experience of loss is the disruption of a narrative. The death of a loved one
causes a revising of the story one has been living. For some, a death means
fashioning a completely new story for one's life. The crisis is personal and
individual, and so is the story about it.

Originally, this chapter illustrated how a pastor from the continent of
Africa brought the resources of the church to bear upon a family facing
the illness and loss of a loved one. The focus was on how the black church,
as a support system, sustained the bereaved family by bringing the unfolding story of God to bear upon the family's needs. This focus on Africa is
essential, particularly when we emphasize the loss of the village and the
need to recover village functions. Since 1991, however, we have become
more aware of catastrophic losses and how devastating they can be. For

example, things have changed about how we view the persistence of natural disaster, human frailty, and evil.

The dynamic behind modernity was an optimism and certainty that life was becoming progressively better and that we would overcome many of the human problems of life through science and human effort. Postmodernity, however, has made us aware that the optimism we have felt was a bit naïve. We have become increasingly aware that science has limitations, human progress takes place in small steps, and the hard-fought gains for liberties in civil and human rights have to be refought in each new generation. In the area of race relations, we became aware that catastrophes like Hurricane Katrina have undermined our confidence in infrastructures designed to protect us. This storm has also made us aware of the reality that racial minorities and the poor are disproportionately affected by natural disaster due to corporate decisions driven by economic interests, racial attitudes, and self-interest politics. Major institutions such as our local, state, and federal governments are ill-prepared for disasters, and our insurance industry, designed to help us recover from losses, is a dismal failure. While Hurricanes Katrina and Rita had an impact on everyone, the consensus is that ethnic and racial minorities and the poor were not only more vulnerable but more affected as well. For example, the levees were stronger and held up better in more affluent areas of New Orleans than in the poorer areas. While this is not a new awareness to the African American community, it is still a hard pill to swallow, and it is disheartening to know that while things have changed racially, they seem to have remained the same. The end result is that we have had to revise our optimistic orientation toward life, and we have had to adopt a more realistic appraisal of human possibility.

From a pastoral care viewpoint, we have had to understand and more fully address the reality of human catastrophe and the role of human lament in recovery from disaster. We have not only had to deal with the individual nature of loss and bereavement, we have had to deal with the public nature of grieving resulting from natural disasters and human evil.

We will return to the subject of public grieving later in this chapter when we explore catastrophic loss.

THE NATURE OF BEREAVEMENT

Bereavement results from the sudden cessation of a close and abiding relationship.[1] Bereavement often elicits negative emotions such as grief or mourning, which come after the death of a person who has had a particular place in one's life. What follows is a generally characteristic pattern as the bereaved tries to fill the void made in his or her life by this loss.

The basic tasks for the bereaved person are to achieve emancipation from bondage to the deceased, readjust to a world in which the deceased is missing, and form new relationships.[2] Another task is to revise and edit one's life story without the deceased. These tasks are difficult because the impact of the death of a loved one is apt to stun bereaved persons to the point of immobilization and disorganization.

Those who suffer grief sometimes want to avoid the pain associated with the experience. After many attempts on the part of the bereaved to avoid that pain, the grieving process itself must be accepted if adequate mourning is to take place. According to Erich Lindemann, once the grief process is accepted, the bereaved begin to deal with the memory of the deceased person, and this, in turn, is followed by relief in tension. Moreover, Lindemann discovered that if others care for the bereaved for four to six weeks, that is an appropriate length of time to help them reach an uncomplicated and undistorted grief reaction.[3]

Certain characteristic symptoms appear in persons suffering bereavement. Lindemann enumerates the following four components of the grief syndrome: (1) body distress; (2) guilt; (3) hostile reactions; (4) loss of patterns of conduct.[4] As a result of the impact of loss, the bereaved might suffer tightness in the throat, shortness of breath, the need to sigh, empty feelings in the stomach, or a lack of muscular power. The senses are altered to the degree that there may be a sense of unreality and a feeling of increased emotional distance from others.

Often, guilt and hostile anger are evident when the bereaved accuse themselves of negligence and look for evidence to corroborate this allegation. Moreover, they may exhibit anger toward relatives and friends of the deceased through a loss of warmth in relationships and a feeling of abandonment on the part of the bereaved.

Death of a loved one disrupts usual patterns of interaction, resulting in a restlessness, an inability to remain in one place, an aimless moving, or a continued search for something to do. There is also a general lack of capacity to initiate and maintain patterns of activity, for the grief sufferer discovers that many of the activities that were done with the deceased or in relationship to the deceased have lost their meaning.

There may be preoccupation with the image and memory of the deceased, often an attempt to deny the death and recover the presence of the lost loved one.[5] There is a yearning or seeking for the loved one, an attempt to achieve reunion with the deceased.[6]

Normal grieving is characterized by three phases. First, the grief sufferers yearn for the lost loved ones and experience anger toward the loved ones for abandoning them. The second phase begins when the bereaved accept the fact that neither yearning nor anger will bring the loved ones back. This leads to despair and disorganization in the lives of the bereaved. Following this phase is a period of reorganization, in which the bereaved turn toward the world and begin to find new relationships and meaning in life. During this period, the grief sufferers either begin the task of revising and editing the old story or begin to develop a new story without the deceased.

During the process of grief work, it is important for the bereaved to experience and express their yearning for and anger toward the deceased. In this way they can give up the deceased and accept the fact that the deceased is gone forever. Only then can they accept the reality that loved ones are separate from themselves and can be lost. Failure to consciously experience and express the yearning for and anger toward the deceased leads to an arresting of the grief process, which eventuates in inappropriate attempts to carry out a reunion with the deceased and, ultimately, to pathological mourning.[7]

BEREAVEMENT MINISTRY: CASE EXAMPLE FROM A BLACK AFRICAN PASTOR IN A BLACK CHURCH

This is a report of an African pastor who ministered to a dying parishioner and the parishioner's family before and after his death. The focus of the pastor's concern was a black male in his late fifties who was dying from cancer. Prior to the discovery of the malignancy, the parishioner had sustained injuries in a serious car accident, and initially, the illness was linked to complications associated with that accident. However, during the period of convalescence it was discovered that he was terminally ill with cancer of the liver. When told of his disease, the parishioner did not accept the prognosis, refusing to admit he was dying. Rather, he insisted that a good job was waiting for him and that he would return to work.

The parishioner's immediate family consisted of a second wife and a son from his first marriage. The second wife did not live with the husband at the time of his illness; the father and son were estranged and had not seen each other for many years.

The parishioner's extended family consisted of two younger sisters who lived in the area and an older sister living in the Deep South. The two younger sisters had a good relationship with their brother, were upset about his illness, and were concerned about his inability to accept the fact that he was dying. The older sister, however, had a much closer relationship with her brother, probably because she had taken care of him during his childhood.

The man's relationship with the pastor was a comfortable one. The pastor had visited the parishioner periodically in the hospital since the accident. The pastor was concerned about the dying man's inability to accept his impending death, and he expressed this concern to the two younger sisters. While talking with the sisters, the pastor discovered that the dying man probably would be much more willing to talk about his problems with his older sister. Therefore, the pastor sent for this sister, and she came as a result of the pastor's initiative. The pastor found that the dying parishioner was able to express his fears to his older sister and finally was able to accept the fact that he was dying. The pastor also contacted the man's son and informed him of his father's condition. As a result of this effort, the son and father were able to establish some form of reconciliation before the father died.

Following the death of the parishioner, the pastor turned his concern to the bereaved family. He discovered that the second wife, the three sisters, and the son had become a fellowship group for one another. The pastor helped strengthen this support system by using the wake and the preparation of the funeral service to facilitate the grief process among the members of the fellowship group. He found that their participation in preparing the funeral service stimulated them to express their feelings concerning the beloved brother, husband, and father.

This African pastor had trained many laypeople in his congregation for times of bereavement. After discovering that many of the parishioners were from the South and the West Indies, and seemed to automatically know what to do in terms of the crisis of loss, he exploited many of those natural leanings and involved these persons in discussion groups surrounding such crises. When there was a need for these persons' services within the congregation, he would call on them to assist others.

The pastor trained these laypeople to share stories from their own lives to encourage the bereaved to share their stories of hurt and pain. He informed them that a brief story from the lives of the caregivers could assist the bereaved to review their own relationships with the deceased and enable feelings of bereavement to be expressed. The pastor warned them, however, to tell their stories in ways that kept the bereaved person's needs for grieving central.

According to the African pastor, much of his knowledge concerning bereavement ministry was a result of his African heritage. Death was accepted as a fact of life in his community in Africa, and many extended family obligations were associated with the death of a loved one and the bereavement process.[8] As "eldest son," the pastor's obligation to the family during the bereavement period had consisted of assisting with funeral arrangements and carrying out the father's wishes concerning the remaining family.

His participation in a consultation group and a seminar on death, dying, and bereavement were also very helpful in shaping his bereavement ministry.

A NARRATIVE REFLECTION ON THE CASE

The Black Pastor as Diagnostician

In the case just described, the pastor became aware that the parishioner refused to accept the fact that he was dying of cancer. This refusal to accept a given reality is called denial. Following the diagnosis, the pastor actively sought to ascertain what sources existed within the family to assist the dying patient through his difficulty and to help him face the reality of death.

The pastor became cognizant of several family resources. The patient's second wife revealed a concern about him and attempted to lend support. In addition, the pastor discovered three sisters, who emerged as the most significant sources of support for the dying patient. An adult son, whose communication with his father had been nonexistent for a period of time, also was considered a potential avenue of support.

Aside from family resources, the pastor assessed resources within the church for support of the dying parishioner. Some members had been trained to be of assistance, and religious ceremonials would provide support. The pastor also became aware that traditions among the members, particularly those from the South and West Indies, provided a set of customs that defined the responsibility of church members and friends to persons in crisis. Thus, a framework existed with which to support the parishioner and ease him in his dying moments. Through the support of the family, the social network, the church and its heritage, and the values of the black subculture that defined the behavior of persons toward others in crises, the pastor recognized the existence of a variety of resources available before and during death, as well as throughout the subsequent bereavement of the family.

Of great help to the black African pastor were the influential cultural patterns in Africa that informed his sensitivity to the role of extended families in ministering to the dying. He used knowledge from his past, and the sensitivities toward the role of support systems acquired from his background in his bereavement ministry to the congregation.

The key to the use of the cultural patterns of the extended family, the support system, and the funeral was the fact that these patterns were embodied in the central narrative of the faith tradition. Those in the extended family were part of God's unfolding story; those in the caring support system of the church were part of God's unfolding story. When these people shared stories of bereavement from their own lives, they included testimonies of God's presence in the midst of death. Moreover, the support system shared a common faith story, which, when shared, held out hope in the midst of tragedy.

The wake and funeral were vehicles for assisting the family through the grieving process. As part of caring, the pastor purposely employed the funeral and the wake to help the bereaved discern God's presence in the midst of their grief. Through the funeral and wake, they could encounter the spacious resources of God's story of grace and hope.

The funeral also laid the groundwork for enabling the bereaved to revise and edit their stories. Images of God's presence in the lives of those who were bereaved in Scripture held out hope for developing new life scenarios. The liturgy of the funeral gave the message that God will assist you in fashioning a new story without the presence of the deceased.

The parishioner in this case had been largely uncommunicative about his condition, with the pastor as well as with two of his sisters. However, after learning of another sister, with whom the brother would be willing to talk, the pastor facilitated the arrival of the third sister, which resulted in the dying patient's discussion of his fears and his acceptance of the fact that he was dying. Moreover, after the pastor brought the dying man and his sister together, they began to share stories of their lives together when they were young. These memories and stories helped to shore up his courage so that he could face the task of dying; they secured the bonds between the dying man and his sister. He was sustained and nurtured by sweet memories and died knowing that his life was worthwhile and that he was loved.

Essential to the narrative understanding of caring ministry to the bereaved is the envisioning of the funeral and the caring as being linked to God's unfolding drama in our lives. God's unfolding story is a drama made up of episodes, scenes, chapters, and a plot. The funeral and the ministry of caring in God's name are miniplots in the midst of God's unfolding macroplot. The macroplot of God involves death and rebirth made possible by Jesus Christ. The salvation drama is made up of dying with Christ and rising with Christ. Therefore, in ministry to the dying and the bereaved, the task is to draw the people into God's salvation drama of death and rebirth.

Reunion of the loved ones with a dying patient is one illustration of how renewal and rebirth are possible despite the imminence of death. In the described case, the resources of God's ongoing story of salvation undergirded and enabled the rebirth of new relationships. The act of being drawn into God's salvation drama offered new possibilities and hope in spite of pain and suffering.

As the bereft are drawn into the salvation drama, the foundation is also being laid for them to begin to revise and edit a different narrative, one that is without the loved one. By being linked with God's unfolding drama of death and rebirth, the bereft find courage to begin a new life and a new narrative without the deceased. A new narrative is begun with hope and expectation, knowing that God is in the revising process.

The Pastor as Mobilizer of Support Systems

The African heritage of the caring pastor in this case made him sensitive to the role of support systems in life transitions. His cultural heritage had built into it traditions of community support and ceremonial practices to aid those in life transitions. These supports and practices gave him a special sensitivity toward knowing how to utilize support systems in bereavement situations with families outside his cultural background.

The major role of the African pastor in the crises of dying and bereavement was to bring the resources of the support system to bear upon the emotional and interpersonal needs of the dying patient and the grieving relatives. By accomplishing this, the pastor (1) provided opportunities for relatives and friends to identify and empathize with one another; (2) provided opportunities to share in a common story of the faith tradition; (3) provided a ritual and worship context for linking and connecting with a meaningful religious plot that brought renewal and rebirth in the midst of suffering; (4) provided a loving and caring group of laypersons and family who facilitated the expression of feelings of grief and mourning; and (5) encouraged the lay caregivers to help the grief sufferers use stories from their own lives as a means of facilitating the grief process.

In order to assist the support system in the case of bereavement and dying, the pastor helped the bereaved and the dying parishioner to maintain significant ties with others, which helped them sustain their emotional and spiritual well-being in the face of death. The support system helped the dying man and his family satisfy their needs for love, affection, and continued participation in meaningful relationships in the midst of suffering.

The use of a support system enabled the pastoral care to be the best within the African and African American church context. The support system helped sustain the dying man during his last days on earth. It brought healing through the renewal of relationships, helped guide the

Callslip Request   1/14/2014 3:46:09 PM

Request date:1/13/2014 02:38 PM
Request ID: 43740
Call Number:253.0899 W757 2008
Item Barcode:

34711001824269

Author: Wimberly, Edward P., 1943-
Title: African American pastoral care / Edward
Enumeration:c.1Year:
Patron Name:Brittani Y Pipes
Patron Barcode:

23693040022236

Patron comment:

Request number:

Route to.   43740
I-Share Library:

Library Pick Up Location:

grief sufferers through the grief process, and enabled the bereaved and the dying man to be linked with the ongoing drama of God's salvation.

RE-VILLAGING ANALYSIS

This revision lifts up the need to reestablish village functions within the African American church as a legitimate twenty-first century function. This case draws on a study of an African minister pastoring an African American church and relating it to support systems originally took place in the late 1970s. It was an illustration of the function of support systems. The goal of the illustration was to be more intentional about making sure these support systems were not lost given the demise of such networks due to cultural trends. My original thinking was that these supportive traditions would not really collapse, believing that the loss of the traditional village would never happen. It has happened, and it is necessary to attend to some of the village functions that were evident in the case as a means to set the theoretical stage for re-creating village functioning today. The main assumption of this section is that a village can never be re-created; however, village functions can be reestablished.

I begin with the emphasis on the indigenous storyteller whose role in the creation of village functions is to assist in communal healing. The communal healing function is to help restore the family relational ties; to use the Bible to evoke the eschatological plot and its practice of drawing persons into the unfolding story of God; to transform people's lives by connecting them with hidden and unconscious resources that lead to resilient strategies in the face of difficulties; and to help people edit the negative beliefs and convictions that might hinder their ability to be resilient. In the case presented above we see illustrated the restoration of relational ties, and we get a glimpse of the use of biblical resources to connect people with the unfolding plot of God. We need to say more about how resilient resources and practices were evoked when stories were elicited, however.

Resilient practices emerge out of the storytelling process itself. In fact, resilient practices are part of the healing function of re-villaging, where the indigenous storyteller facilitates the storytelling process, and from the storytelling process new insights are stimulated for bouncing back from loss. In our publication *The Winds of Promise: Building and Sustaining Clergy Families* my wife and I define resilient practices as engaging in the storytelling process from which people are able to gain access to hidden and unused opportunities for managing life's twists and turns.[9] Spiritual lifelines often emerge from our storytelling that provide opportunities to see the next steps in moving through difficulties that we face in life. This was evident when the family members became aware of God's plot of reconciliation and healing unfolding in their lives so that old relationships could be reestablished. While no actual biblical story was named in the case, they nonetheless became aware of an active and connecting dynamic at work that enabled them to transcend past hurts and problems. This dynamic force was already at work, but it was outside their awareness, and the storytelling enabled them to become aware and connect with it. It was this previously hidden dynamic that enabled them to reconnect with each other and to find support for each other in the dying process and in the grief that they were experiencing.

CATASTROPHIC LOSS

In addition to the private grief of human beings, events like the Columbine shootings in Colorado in 1999, the 9/11 attacks, and the Katrina catastrophe of 2005 have made us aware that grief has a public side. The public nature of grief has not been satisfactorily addressed by pastoral care and counseling as a discipline. In an article by Larry Graham entitled "Pastoral Theology and Catastrophic Disaster" delivered at the Society of Pastoral Theology in June 2006, Graham points out that such events as the Columbine shootings, 9/11, and Katrina forced us to struggle with how caregivers can help themselves and others come to terms with the corporate and public dimensions of grief and loss, which had been ignored in pastoral theology. Pastoral care normally confined its thinking about grief and loss to the personal and private realm. Thus, Larry Graham raises the concern of how pastors and pastoral theologians can rethink the public and corporate nature of loss and grief. Toward this end, Graham lifts up several practices, and one such practice is the role of lament as a resilient practice.

In Graham's exposition of lament, he credits a phone conversation with me for introducing the meaning of lament. In my books, *Claiming God, Reclaiming Dignity: African American Pastoral Care and Counseling* and *The Winds of Promise: Building and Sustaining Clergy Families*, I define lament as crying out and complaining to God about our current predicament, being honest about God's role in the cause of such predicaments, and expecting God to respond. Lament as an ancient biblical practice was designed to draw people into conversation with God so that the resilient resources that God has for bouncing back from catastrophic circumstances can be activated. Lament actively questions God's role in causing the catastrophe, but such complaints are not considered blasphemy. Rather, it is considered an appropriate response to helplessness and a genuine invitation for God to be present in the lives of those who suffer. In blasphemy, there is no genuine acknowledgment of God's existence or desire to be engaged with God.

Of significance is the reality that public and corporate lament is a resilient practice. First, lament provides connection with God, who is the ultimate source of new opportunities and hidden resources for bouncing back from loss, devastation, and catastrophe. Second, in addition, public and corporate grieving are re-villaging practices as well. They assist in the symbolic function of re-villaging by bringing to life certain narratives, metaphors, and images that embody the spiritual resources of the faith traditions. See, for example, the many psalms of lament and the laments found in the Book of Job. There is also the re-villaging public aspect of the ritualistic recitation of the psalms of lament provided in biblical tradition. Third, public and corporate lament perform the maintenance function of securing relational ties needed to overcome devastation. Fourth, corporate public lament assists in the reparative function, so that healing the hurt and brokenness of those affected by catastrophe can take place. Finally, lament enables the spiritual and relational values of the faith tradition to be mediated to those who have faced catastrophe. This is the mediation function.

Indeed, the role of the pastor as indigenous storyteller is critical in times of catastrophe. The symbolic role of the black preacher as village leader is essential during catastrophe as well as during the recovery phase after catastrophe. One thinks of the role that the Reverend Lance Eden, pastor of First Street United Methodist Church in New Orleans, played during Katrina as well as into the recovery phase. During Sunday morning worship he led his congregation and the many volunteers who came from all around the United States in public and corporate lament during public worship. Not only this, he also led his congregation and volunteers in restoring the homes that were salvageable and helped reestablish communal networks that Katrina disrupted. *Ebony Magazine* and *Colors Magazine* acknowledged his leadership efforts during the Katrina recovery. In fact, the November 2005 issue of *Colors Magazine* featured an article on Eden's work entitled "After the Storm: Special Report from the Gulf Coast."[10]

The article in *Colors Magazine* lifts up, in effect, Eden's role as indigenous storyteller in the re-villaging and recovery effort in New Orleans. It says:

> In the part of town known as Indian Village, Lance Eden offers a history lesson about the area his family calls home. Serious and thoughtful, all who speak of Eden see a great leader in the making. Someone who is wise enough to be able to say he doesn't know and confident enough to take the lead when the need arises. Eden sees the preservation of his family history as part of his responsibility not just to his kin but to the history of Slidell. The history of his family stretches back centuries, and

as a history buff, he has taken to compiling and keeping stories for future generations.[11]

The life of the Reverend Lance Eden as minister and indigenous story-teller is an illustration of how the African American tradition re-creates itself over and over again. While the tangible evidence of a family's life such as mementoes and pictures were lost in many cases, the storytelling traditions and re-villaging functions continue as the stories are still retold. The symbolic role of African American preachers is alive and well as the work of Lance Eden reveals. We who taught Lance at Interdenominational Theological Center and helped form him spiritually and professionally are very proud of his work. At the age of 27, he has the wisdom and maturity of a much older, seasoned minister. We are happy that the tradition of the indigenous storyteller continues in our graduates.

PASTORAL CARE AND LIFE CRISES

BIRTH, ADOLESCENCE, YOUNG ADULTHOOD, MIDDLE ADULTHOOD, AND OLDER ADULTHOOD

Members of the church community who are facing predictable life transitions often call on black pastors and laypeople. These transitions that occur throughout the life cycle sometimes are referred to as developmental crises. These crises usually are growth opportunities; and while they may present some difficulties for those who face them, pastors and caring laypeople can respond with empathy and compassion in ways that help those in crisis to grow.

Life crises are no longer as predictable as in the past. The work of developmental psychologist Erik Erikson from the 1950s dominated the modern understanding of life crises. Although he introduced an understanding of how the sociohistorical and cultural context influenced the human life cycle, the world of the 1950s and 1960s is vastly different from today's. The life cycle in the 1979 book and the later revision of 1991 assumed the worldview of a stable life cycle. Thus, the earlier editions of this work were not written with the weakening of cross-generational ties in view. Contemporary contextual conditions dictate that we explore the human life cycle in light of the impact of current sociohistorical and cultural factors.

The focus in this chapter is on ways the black pastor and caring laypeople can respond to contemporary life-cycle transitions through the use of a narrative approach. Black pastors, as well as laity, can draw upon the rich story resource of their own lives and of Scripture and bring it to bear upon the lives of persons facing life transitions.

LIFE TRANSITIONS

Life transitions, as crises, are periods when individuals face obstacles brought on by normal changes from within the person. These are obstacles that cannot be resolved by the customary ways of resolving crises.[1] Factors that contribute to the onset of these developmental crises include the birth of a child, a child entering school for the first time, the onset of adolescence, a young adult leaving home, marriage, and the onset of middle and old age. These times are typically characterized by brief periods of increased tension, periods of risk when customary ways of resolving problems do not work, the seeking of help from significant others to resolve the crisis, and the trying of new ways to come to grips with the new challenge. Successfully coming to grips with the life crisis involves (1) facing the problem head-on; (2) working on the various emotional and social tasks presented by the problem; (3) coming to some understanding of what one is experiencing; and (4) talking with caring others about the situation.

Each life transition has its own dynamics and patterns. Black pastors and laity can benefit from understanding some predictable crises and the tasks people must accomplish when facing these crises.

THE LIFE CYCLE AND THE TWENTY-FIRST CENTURY

This chapter considers the sociocultural and historical context affecting the life cycle of African American individuals, marriages, and families. As in previous chapters, the presupposition is that sociocultural and historical contexts have changed and that the collapse of the village and its functions has taken place within the African American family and extended family. These changes have tremendous consequences for the life cycle of African Americans. The main sociocultural and historical consequence is that many factors "have lessened the cross-generational ties that are needed for African Americans and other ethnic groups to successfully negotiate life-cycle tasks and transitions."[2] Among these factors are a high-tech economy; relocation of industrial jobs to poorer countries, which lessens employment opportunities; the prevalence of consumer and marketing values; the loosening of generational ties; the disappearing of support systems; and continued racial discrimination.[3] Traditional African American communal values such as strong family-oriented ties, reverence for elders, caring for children, a deep sense of spirituality, and a conviction that life is sacred have eroded; and a prevailing sense of nihilism or loss of a sense of meaning and purpose prevail. The end result is the lessening of the ability to negotiate successfully life-cycle tasks and transitions. There is a loss of relational skills that are essential to maintain close and intimate relationships and to build on previous stages of the life cycle.[4]

Perhaps the most significant problem affecting the life cycle is the loss of the ability to participate in cross-generational relationships. The assumption is "that participation in cross-generational relationships serves to mentor children, youth, and young adults throughout the life cycle in the wisdom of past generations and the communal traditions conveyed through ritual."[5] Factors such as leaving the rural areas, living mostly in urban areas, and the prevalence of electronic media have replaced the rational settings for raising children. The end result is that youth and young adults have lost the capacity to participate in cross-generational relationships and have become isolated and can be termed "relational refugees." The ability to participate in meaningful relationships is essential throughout the life cycle, and the failure to have such relationships severely cripples our ability to negotiate life-cycle tasks.

One key result of the loss of generational ties is the capacity of youth, young adults, and adults to develop the necessary emotional and social skills to sustain close and intimate relationships.[6] Participation in cross-generational relationships mentors children, youth, and young adults throughout the life cycle in the wisdom of previous generations and the communal realities undergirding the life of communities. Elders are the primary socializing agents of cultures, and without cross-generational relationships, skills necessary for traversing life-cycle transitions are lacking. The point is that we must restore the village functions that support how we move successfully through the life cycle.

Birth as a Life Crisis

Pregnancy is a crisis for the pregnant mother as well as for those whose lives are affected by the pregnancy. Pregnancy disrupts the ordinary ways the mother thinks, feels, and relates. Emotional upsets, role changes, and communication problems must be worked through.

The changes that take place within the expectant mother are normal, but they can cause tension with significant others. Metabolic changes can cause the expectant mother to experience mood swings. Concerns that may arise between the expectant mother and her own mother may cause tension. The expectant mother's preoccupation with the pregnancy can cause the expectant father to feel left out. Sometimes unresolved marital issues may surface. Any unresolved issues the mother has with sexuality also may surface and cause tension. New roles, as well as adjustments to new circumstances, are required of all involved.

These examples of changes brought on by pregnancy show that it is a predicable and normal life crisis. It requires the expectant mother and significant others to make changes in their lives and attitudes. And it is significant that pregnancy provides an opportunity for the pastor and caring persons to respond with empathy and care.

The church takes a significant role when the pastor and caring members enable it to use its natural faith tradition to help draw the expectant mother and significant others into the unfolding story of God. For churches that baptize infants, baptism is an important means of incorporating the entire family into God's ongoing story. For churches that dedicate infants, with emphasis on believers' baptisms, this also is a way to draw the child and the family into God's drama unfolding in the midst of the church. Preparation for baptism or dedication prior to the birth can help the expectant family discern the upcoming event as part of God's unfolding drama.

The role of the pastor and caring laypeople is to help those involved (1) understand what is taking place as a result of the pregnancy; (2) facilitate the expression and acceptance of the feelings of those whose lives are directly affected; and (3) help those involved to mobilize resources for responding positively to the crisis. Stories can be used at any of these points to assist in the resolution of the crisis. This is illustrated well by the following case illustration of a pastor who responds to a husband whose wife is pregnant for the first time.

Jane was in the fifth month of pregnancy, the second trimester. James went to the pastor very perplexed because he could not predict his wife's moods, and he resented the fact that she refused sexual relations with him more often since she had been pregnant. He complained that she was always sick and wanted him to wait on her, that the house never looked right, and that she always seemed tired.

The pastor discovered in their conversation that James had no understanding about the nature of pregnancy or about what pregnant women normally experience. He was not aware that pregnancy brought on mood swings and new psychological and emotional tasks for the expectant mother. He had no knowledge of how to be supportive of his wife. James was facing a crisis and needed the help of his pastor. The pastor knew that

James needed to understand pregnancy as a life crisis. James also needed to know that his wife's reactions were a normal part of bringing a new life into the world and that his role as a supportive and empathic mate was essential for Jane to feel secure in her pregnancy.

The pastor spent time listening to James and allowed him to express his resentment and confusion without censoring those feelings. He wanted James to be comfortable and to look on the pastor as a friend. The pastor felt this was an essential foundation for the time when he would help James understand his wife's needs and how he could respond to them.

The pastor decided to relate a scenario from his own experience as a husband who had faced the crisis of birth for the first time. His goals for relating the story were to foster increased empathy, to help James identify with the pastor's plight as a way to understand his own plight, and to enable James to identify with the solution the pastor had brought to the crisis. The pastor hoped that through the scenario James would come to understand his wife's needs better and be able to respond supportively.

The pastor told James that as a young man, he had never been around a pregnant woman. His father never mentioned anything about the nature of pregnancy or about how a male should respond; his peers were not available, since he had cut himself off from them when he married. Rather, the pastor had to learn the hard way, by discovering things on his own through reading. In fact, he had no resources other than what he read. The pastor told James that he was quite surprised to learn that what his wife was experiencing was normal. Once he, the pastor, understood what was happening, he was able to be more caring toward his wife. He felt that when he had not known about natural mood swings, he had been resentful, but the resentment disappeared when he understood the nature of pregnancy.

After James heard the pastor's story, he was able to see clearly his wife's needs and that he needed to be supportive. The pastor's skillful use of his own life experience enabled James to understand his own crisis. It helped him visualize the different role he needed to play, to clear up negative perceptions, and to work through negative feelings.

From this case illustration, it is obvious that the cross-generational connections were absent for this couple, especially for the expectant father. In a real sense, the pastor became a surrogate or substitute for the cross-generational village, functioning to mediate wisdom. In the traditional village, it was the support system made up of aunts and uncles that provided the wisdom for dealing with pregnancy and becoming expectant parents. The transmission of such wisdom is still important, as the case reveals, but it was carried out by the pastor.

No doubt the pastor had either been raised in a rural culture or he had been educated in a culturally sensitive model of psychology that emphasized the use of support systems in life transitions. Just as the pastor had knowledge of cultural traditions related to life transitions, congregations also need to be educated in such traditions as part of the restoration of village functions. Thus, an effort to educate congregational support systems in village functions during life transitions is essential in the twenty-first century.

Not only is it important to educate congregational support systems in the twenty-first century, it is absolutely mandatory to be aware of the issues facing African American fathers as we prepare to restore the village functions. Recent studies show that African American men are becoming increasingly disconnected from their communal roots. For example, Erik Eckholm in an article in the *New York Times*, March 20, 2006, entitled "Plight Deepens for Black Men, Studies Warn," says the following:

> Black men in the United States face a far more dire situation than is portrayed by common employment and education statistics, a flurry of new scholarly studies warn, and it has worsened in recent years even as an economic boom and a welfare overhaul have brought gains to black women and other groups.[7]

He indicates that a large group of poorly educated black men are becoming what some have called "relational refugees," or men who are becoming increasingly disconnected from mainstream society.[8] The problems that the article enumerates relate to inner cities and include early school dropout rates, legal problems, and high incarceration rates, along with criminal activity, joblessness/unemployment, substance abuse and addiction, violence of all kinds, absent parents, terrible schools, the breakdown of families at the core, and the absence of life skills. A growing number of programs advocate teaching life skills such as parenting, conflict resolution, and character-building, along with teaching job skills.

This article in the *New York Times*[9] is based on research done by the Urban Institute in Washington, D.C., and the publications that it produces through its Urban Institute Press. The Urban Institute is a non-partisan think tank, and its press publishes scholarly books on domestic social issues and policy. Two publications are key for providing the latest information on African American males and the disconnections taking place with them. The first is by Ronald Mincy, and it is entitled *Black Males Left Behind.*[10] The second is by Peter Edelman, Harry Holzer, and Paul Offner, and it is entitled *Reconnecting Disadvantaged Young Men.*[11]

The apparent disconnection seems to be more common for young men, particularly African American and low-income young men, than for young women. The effort to reconnect these men to their families through life skills education is the goal of this proposal. *The basic approach assumes that one way to reconnect African American males to the economic mainstream and the labor force is through reconnecting them to their families. Becoming connected relationally is the major source of motivation for self-improvement.*

Given the need, there are major activities that need to take place as the black church seeks to restore the village functions and get African American men connected. These activities include: (1) providing marital and family life educational enrichment for fathers and their families; (2) developing marital and family life enrichment curriculum that will target African American men and their families from the low economic strata; (3) evaluating the usefulness of a narrative storytelling method of marital and family enrichment for reconnecting African American men to their families; and (4) establishing best practices emerging from the marital and family enrichment activities.

The support that people need to transcend the conditions in which they live takes the entire village. Disconnections and loss of cross-generational connections as the result of advances in technology and lack of sanctioned support for nurturing and caring values across generations by the wider culture devastate African Americans. In fact, one of the impacts has to do with their influence on the African American life cycle. In most cases, these factors disrupt it and make it harder for us to resolve life-cycle tasks. Thus, the black church must step up to meet this need, and this is especially important for expectant African American fathers.

Adolescence as a Life Crisis

Adolescence is a shaky bridge between childhood and adulthood, a predictable life crisis brought on by physiological changes. The major task of adolescents is to correlate the way they see themselves as persons with the way others see them. During this period of identity formation, both boys and girls begin to negotiate who they are apart from others as well as in relationship to others. It is a time of finding one's own place in the world and developing the kinds of skills needed for social and economic well-being. Some problems for black youths are a result of the traditional racial climate and the reliability of family and extended family support.

One of the major tasks of adolescence is learning to negotiate the strong impulses that are welling up inside. The task involves developing a mature sexual identity and controlling one's sexual impulses in healthy and constructive ways. The major difficulty that faces contemporary adolescents is the absence of a language of sexuality for youth that conveys strong relational values and encourages the postponing of sexual expression. Relational values refer to learning the value of friendship and the worth of persons of the opposite sex as objects of love and respect, rather than as objects for sexual gratification. Pastoral care from the perspective of relational values helps youths put sex in the context of marriage, as an expression of love, respect, and responsibility.

Key for our lives in the twenty-first century is understanding that we are living in a culture here in the United States that targets black youth for consumer buying using sex and violence as a means to promote their spending.[12] Youth are bombarded by messages whose goal is to recruit them into spending their money on fashions and music appealing to their needs for significance with their peers. Of course, sex is a major appeal in the music as well as in the fashion market. The challenge for black youth according to Richelle B. White in *Daughters of Imani* is developing the critical skills necessary to make decisions not only on what to buy but also on how to live. White says that youth, and especially young Christian women, need the skills to assess and critique a culture of promiscuity.[13] Youth need to learn to process cultural images that often lead them into harmful sexual self-images and practices. Moreover, youth need an open environment where sexuality can be openly discussed and where youth can be mentored and nurtured by older women and men. The cross-generational dimension of this discussion is essential.

Closely connected to a culture of promiscuity and consumerism is the danger of sexual addiction. This is a particular problem for budding adolescents in the United States and for African American youth in particular. In a study of 600 junior high American youth, 91 percent of the boys and 83 percent of the girls indicated that they had seen X-rated hard-core pornography.[14] The point is that our youth are vulnerable to being recruited into a life of addiction given the fact that the Internet is a welcoming medium for curious youth. Along with the breakup of the cross-generational village as well as the increasing disconnection taking place from relationships, sex becomes the medicine of choice for persons to use as a substitute for relationships. Sex is sought as a medication for alienation and for a people that are increasingly becoming relational refugees cut off from significant relationships. Of course, the turn to sex as a way to medicate alienation and relationship wounds fuels the consumer-oriented culture's use of sex to sell material goods.

A culture of promiscuity and of addiction fuels the risk of being exposed to HIV/AIDS and other sexually transmitted diseases. Moreover, promiscuity and addiction among adolescents also make youth vulnerable to life-cycle problems for which they are not prepared. One of the problems is that youth are exposed to problems with which they are emotionally ill-equipped to handle. These problems not only include teen pregnancy; they also include the disruption of key life-cycle emotional tasks, which both adolescent boys and girls must accomplish. Prematurely engaging in sexual activity can disrupt the process of internalizing significant others, which begins at birth and continues through identity formation in adolescence and beyond in some cases. Psychiatrist and sex therapist David Schnarch points out that children and youth need good experiences with primary figures in their lives so that they can sustain resilient and meaningful attachments in their adult lives.[15] Such a capacity for attachment emerges in the first three to four years of life according to Schnarch, and these attachments lay the groundwork for a strong sense of self, the capacity for creativity, sexual involvement, and self-assertion. It has been my experience as a pastoral counselor that youth with good experiences postpone sexual activity into young adulthood, and those without such good experiences with primary figures in their lives often engage in sexual activities before they are emotionally ready. Premature engagement in sexual intercourse can interrupt and disrupt the groundwork needed to increase one's relational potential for future sexual involvement.

My presupposition is that sexual intercourse is one of the deepest forms of human communication of the self, and it is also a process of taking into the self another person who becomes part of one's own personality. Thus, sexual intercourse requires a great deal of readiness, and it cannot be casual.

The disruption of the internalized good experiences with nurturing primary figures was graphically demonstrated by one of my counselees who had been promiscuous since her mid-teens. Not all of her experiences with her primary nurturing figures were good, especially with regard to her father. Consequently, she turned to other persons for nurture and care, and some of them misused her for their own sexual pleasure. From the time of her mid-teens to twenty-three years of age, she engaged in promiscuous sex. Tired of dealing with the problems associated with promiscuous sex, she decided to become celibate as part of her Christian walk. She said she was not ready for what happened when she became celibate. What occurred was that she had to exorcise each personality that she had ever slept with since her teen years, and this was hard work and took over a year. She said that she did not ever want to repeat this process again.

Indeed, sexual relationships affect human beings, including males, at a deep level. Our culture does not talk about this level of emotional and spiritual connecting, and we do our young people a disservice as a result. Our youth need the time during adolescence to complete the task of maturing by having a safe and caring environment of supportive primary figures. African American pastoral care can promote such an understanding of sexuality espoused in this chapter. A narrative approach to the language of sexuality is one approach.

The narrative approach lends itself well to helping youths develop a language of sexuality. Narrative, by its very nature, encourages relationships. The best way to teach the language of sexuality is for parents to share with their children the struggles they underwent as youths.

I once conducted an intergenerational worship service for youths and their parents. I encouraged the parents to share with their children what it was like for them as teenagers. I asked them to tell of the conflict that existed between them and their parents, what the peer morality was like at that time, the fears they had in dating, and the courting strategies they used.

One grandmother about seventy-five years of age told that when she was reared in Alabama in the early 1890s, kids did not have the kind of freedom they have today. She had several brothers and sisters, and her parents wanted to know her whereabouts at all times, though the boys had a little more freedom than the girls. She also described the rules for dating: boys could visit her only when one of her parents was home. There were dances, but her parents had to know who was sponsoring the dance before they would allow her to go. If her parents did not have confidence in the person or group holding the dance, she was not permitted to attend. She said that she had felt her parents were too strict, and she could hardly wait until she was an adult so that she could be free of her parents' domination.

The pastoral care goals of this exercise were to (1) foster better relationships between the generations; (2) lay a positive foundation for open relationships between parents; (3) help youths feel they were understood by their parents; and (4) create a language of sexuality that includes more than sexual intercourse. Narrative sharing helped accomplish this. That is, by relating and sharing stories about their lives as teenagers, the parents helped the youths envision the true tasks of adolescent growth. Moreover, the youths realized that sexual intercourse is not the answer to the complex growth issues involved in establishing identity. Black men, and fathers in particular, need to be part of this kind of narrative sharing so that black males can learn that an adolescent's identity needs are more complex than the making of babies.

Pastoral care with adolescents is intergenerational. Black youth today have turned to peers as though peers are the family. This is an important dimension of gang activity in urban areas, and the fostering of better relationships between parents and youths through narrative pastoral care can provide an alternative. Pastoral care from an intergenerational perspective can help the youths feel that they are part of the family and do not need to depend totally on the peer group for support. Although the peer group is essential for the accomplishment of some tasks, positive relationships between a youth and his or her parents assist greatly in establishing adolescent identity.

Young Adulthood as a Life Crisis

Young adulthood marks the onset of maturity physically, psychologically, and socially. The young adult's physical maturation is complete. If the person has successfully negotiated the previous life-cycle transition and accompanying tasks, his or her identity as a separate, yet significantly related person, has a firm foundation; and the person has had a good chance to develop basic skills of communicating and getting along with others.

The 1991 edition of this work took the relational dimensions needed to make successful life-cycle transitions from one stage to the next for granted. Yet, it is possible to see in the 1991 edition that the problems associated with loss of cross-generational ties and their impact on the life cycle were already present. More precisely, the evidence of being disconnected was evident, though it was not as pronounced as it is today. Today, the evidence of disconnection of people, particularly African American men, is in; and it is an error to proceed believing that the relational connections that characterized past African American families are still in full force.

Developmental psychology, particularly that following the Erik Erikson model, has shown that the relational and emotional dimensions within each life-cycle period must be addressed. The work associated with the Eriksonian model was built on the epigenetic model inherited from Freudian psychology, where certain tasks were associated with the idea that there was a ripe time for emergence for specific tasks. In this theory certain developmental tasks emerge according to appropriate age-related predetermined times related to genetics and, consequently, physiology. Freud and Erikson focused their developmental theory on the physiology of human growth.[16] According to this epigenetic theory, failure to address the appropriate developmental task at the time of its origin or manifestation has grave consequences for the development of the personality.

Contemporary developmental theory assumes that there is a physiological timing in the emergence of developmental tasks, but these more recent theories pay attention to the failure to form inner relationships or representations by internalizing the primary parental figures in our lives. Failure to form inner relationships by appropriately internalizing our primary parental figures is one of the contemporary sources of failure to respond to the physiological origin of the tasks when they first appear.

Object relations theory and Self Psychology both help us understand the impact that failure to form the right kinds of inner relationships has on the life cycle. Object relations theory focuses on internalized relationships with significant others early in our lives, and these relationships eventually become a source of our identity, our feelings about our self-worth and value, as well as a template with which the personality screens new experiences.[17] Thus, this template becomes a powerful dynamic force governing behavior and experience. Our templates become part of our narrative memory or stories that shape our lives, and as such these inner templates have an impact on the life cycle.

My book *Relational Refugees* gives numerous examples of those whose early lives have been affected by inadequate internalized relationships, and the end result is a delay and distortion of life-cycle tasks. Drawing on the adolescent boy, Benji, in Alice Childress's *A Hero Ain't Nothin but a Sandwich*, I conclude that Benji's biological father's abandonment of him in earlier years resulted in the failure to internalize a template that would allow other males into his life to mentor him through adolescence.[18] With regard to adolescent girls, I drew on Toni Morrison's novel *The Bluest Eye*, where Pecola, an adolescent girl, eventually put out her eyes because she did not have blue eyes like some white teenage girls.[19] Her inner template, which did not allow her to see herself as worthwhile and beautiful, was developed out of internalizing her father's negative and abusive behavior toward her. Thus, her internalized negative self-image kept her from experiencing self-love, and she became a relational refugee as a result.

The major tasks of young adulthood include making important choices. First, young adults must develop skills for surviving economically. Second, they must decide whether to remain single or marry and whether to establish a family. Third, they must decide what role religion will play in their lives. Finally, they must find their own way in the world and make their contributions to the world.

Increasingly, the pastoral care concerns of black young adults are intergenerational family concerns. It does appear that the launching of black young adults into full participation in society requires positive contact with and support from the older generation. For socioeconomic and emotional reasons, many African American, as well as Caucasian, young adults are postponing entrance into full participation in the major tasks of young adulthood. I have heard many comments by parents of young adults between the ages of eighteen and thirty, wondering when their children will finally leave home and establish their own lives. Although it is an expectation of American culture that young adults leave home and begin to make their own way in society, these expectations are being altered by the reality of what some are now calling the "postponed generation." Many young adults feel ill-equipped emotionally to face the world. Many feel they do not *yet* have all the resources from the parental home needed to negotiate in the world.

The phenomenon of postponed leaving of the home is an indication of the need for re-parenting or the need to hang around home because the reality is that there is no village to sustain the positive internalized relationships that one has already developed. Developmentally, there is the need to have sustained cross-generational relationships so that the inner positive template can stay intact. The emotional fear of the postponed generation is the fear that such relationships are rare.

The idea of the postponed generation was already part of the 1991 edition of this work. What is new, however, is that those cross-generational relationships are more shattered now than in the past. One implication is that pastoral care must begin to address the need to help people create more cross-generational relationships intentionally, and the other is that there will be increased need for long-term and in-depth pastoral counseling for those who have not internalized adequate positive primary parental figures.

Another implication is that each stage of the life cycle presents opportunities to resolve issues and accomplish tasks that were not present in the earlier stages. Thus, establishing cross-generational relationships with blood kin along with networks of close relationships can help resolve some issues related to internalizing others who can somehow become surrogate parental figures. Moreover, getting into therapy is also important, particularly if the parental internalizations are punitive or very weak.

Pastoral care from a narrative perspective involves the creation of a context in which young adults and their parents can share stories concerning the postponing of the launch into adulthood. The generations seem to have difficulty communicating because the postponed launch is a new phenomenon that has emerged since the 1970s. Creating an atmosphere where stories are shared can help bridge the gap between the generations.

One reason for the postponed generation is that children born after 1960 feel less parented than those of previous generations. Within the African American community, the foundations of the black extended family are crumbling, single-parent families are on the increase, and even in a two-parent home both parents must work if the family is to survive economically. These factors contribute to the feelings of not being adequately parented. Also, many young adults feel that they were abandoned by their parents and given to others, particularly the school, to be raised. Pastoral care for these young adults must take narrative seriously.

The specific tasks for narrative pastoral care with young adults include establishing an atmosphere where parents and young adults feel free to share their stories; enabling the young adult to share what it is like to face the outside world; enabling the parents to share stories of their own launching and the kinds of support they had; and allowing the pastor to share his or her own stories of launching. The ultimate goal for this intergenerational narrative approach is to provide the necessary bonding between the generations and the adequate parenting that has been lacking. Bonding between generations can provide the emotional support needed by young adults to enable them to remain emotionally whole as they negotiate in the world. Narrative sharing is the most natural means of bonding at this stage, since it enables the young adult to remain a mature person who is leaving home. The following example illustrates how to create a context of narrative sharing across generations.

A mother, whose newly married son lived at home because of financial reasons, sought the pastor's help. Both parents had had reservations but had reluctantly agreed to participate in this new arrangement after their son convinced them that the problems would be minimal. However, they had made no effort to talk about how to handle conflict, nor had they discussed how a new arrangement with a daughter-in-law in the home might affect them. The mother felt that she had put forth her best effort but had become a prisoner in her own home. She wanted out of the arrangement.

The pastor listened and empathized with the mother. He shared with her the similar problem his own parents had with his younger brother. The pastor was realistic with the mother about the nature of the problem. Such an arrangement, he felt, should be only temporary because there was so much conflict.

When the mother asked the pastor how she could address the problem, he suggested that she be frank with her son and daughter-in-law. When the pastor asked the mother how her husband felt about this, she said that he shared her feelings. She then asked the pastor if he could be with her and her husband as they spoke with their son and his wife. The pastor agreed, explaining that his role would be to help all of them share their feelings and attempt to solve the problem as they explored alternatives.

Intergenerational support through narrative sharing is essential in order for the young adult to accomplish the tasks of being a young adult. I have illustrated how a narrative approach can address the concern of leaving home. That approach also can address other concerns of the young adult; two of these, premarriage and marriage, will be addressed in the next chapter.

Another significant concern is religion, which becomes dominant around the transition age of thirty, when young adulthood is coming to an end. The adult is settling down, and part of settling down is giving attention to the role one will play in the faith drama or story. Concern for one's spiritual roots is present during young adulthood, but the transition age of thirty, generally accompanied by full launching into the world, stimulates the need to give attention to one's spiritual basis.

Pastoral care during this transition age can take on a spiritual orientation. Here the pastor listens to the stories of the adult and helps the person discern God's presence and story working in his or her life. Pastors over age thirty can draw on their own personal experiences of God at that age as a means of facilitating discernment. Stories from others who discerned God's story and presence during the age-thirty transition can also be shared.

Middle Adulthood as a Life Crisis

Here again, there may be persons entering middle years with re-parenting needs related to the absence of strong and nurturing internalizations or the presence of abusive or punitive ones. In this life-cycle stage there is still opportunity to make cross-generational connections and engage in pastoral psychotherapy to shore up this deficit.

Middle adulthood is the period between thirty-five and fifty-five when we begin to decline physically, when we must reorient our dreams in life, and when we must establish a transcendent basis for identity. The major crisis in midlife is to find one's place in a culture that values youth more than seasoned wisdom. The dominant narrative concern of those in midlife is the search for a more lasting story and plot that will enable them to transcend a culture that is hostile to them.

Pastoral care in midlife is concerned with assisting midlifers to discern the appropriate scenario, story, or plot that will form the basis of their character as they face the second half of life. Pastoral care during midlife helps persons anchor their lives in a faith story that will enable them to find a lasting basis for self. This narrative basis must be the source of midlifers' meaning and purpose. It must give them a sense of making a significant contribution to life, despite unfulfilled dreams, loss of youth, and decreasing significance in the job market.

The needs of a lasting narrative basis in midlife are true for both black males and black females. Females, however, may have an advantage over men in resolving the midlife crisis, since black women, as a whole, have been attending to their need for a religious or spiritual basis for identity throughout adulthood. This gender difference is supported by a culture that expects women to maintain their relatedness with one another and with God. Men, on the other hand, are expected to deny their need for others and for relatedness to God. They are expected to be self-sufficient, to make their way as rugged individualists. As a result, black men lag far behind black women in developing a lasting basis of identity in spiritual sources.

Because black men cannot ignore the need for a spiritual source of identity at midlife, many do begin to turn toward spiritual things at this stage. They become more concerned about relationships with significant others, about building more lasting relationships with the next generation, and about leaving the world a better place for their offspring. Finally, they concern themselves with being better mates to their spouses. In order to accomplish these concerns, they need a transcendent story on which to base their lives.

Black women in midlife need to shore up the narrative basis of their identity in the faith story. While relatedness is not the major concern, increased concern for making it in the world emerges. This is especially true for those who have given their primary attention to raising children. Once the children are launched, many black women turn their interest toward the work world. But for many black mothers who raise children at the same time they are working outside the home, launching children still presents a real obstacle in midlife.

Nonmothers and never-married black women also have a need to renew the narrative and spiritual bases of their identities. Like men, their interests may have been predominantly in the work world, but those with no children and those who never married still have a better balance between their work or career identities and their spiritual identities than do black men.

From a narrative perspective, pastoral care to both men and women in midlife involves helping them return to the stories of childhood, especially the faith stories. The successful outcome of the midlife crisis comes when midlifers rediscover faith stories on which they were raised. Moreover, the caregiver will need to help these midlifers allow these stories to take initiative in their lives. This means helping them retell the stories of old and discern how those stories are shaping their lives in the present.

During midlife our children are launched, but it is also a time when we must care for the past generation. I am reminded of one middle-aged man who had a successful career but had never paid much attention to his parents. Now, he had begun to worry about them. He told me he had discovered an increased need to care for his aging parents in a very dramatic way.

He had awakened early one morning with the Scripture Mark 7:7 on his mind. He did not remember ever encountering the verse before, and he ran to his Bible and began to read, beginning with verse 7. He read through to verse 13 and discovered that this verse had to do with honoring mother and father. He did some reading of commentaries at the church library and realized that the meaning of the passage had to do with neglect of one's parents. This helped convince him of his own neglect, made him aware of his deep spiritual roots, and helped him rediscover a neglected part of his spiritual life. He told me that he was committing himself to Bible study and prayer at his church, so that he could further discover a spiritual resource he had encountered when the Scripture passage came to his mind.

Midlifers need to talk with someone who understands their need for a transcendent resource. The caregiver's task is to enter peoples' stories and help them see God's story at work in their lives. If the caregivers have been through midlife, they can share their own stories. If the caregivers are younger, telling stories they have encountered about midlife can be helpful. The basic assumption in the narrative approach to midlife is that God's story is at work in these peoples' lives, and the caregiver's role is to help the midlifer become aware of this.

Older Adulthood as a Life Crisis

It is possible for older adults to have unresolved needs for nurturing and care, which can be addressed through relationships with peers. Moreover, this is a time for connecting with blood relatives from earlier generations. It is also a time to mourn past losses but also to take advantage of the opportunity to create relationships with the younger generation in order to pass on wisdom. Some elders also engage in group therapy as well as in personal therapy.

The process of developing a long-lasting faith story on which to build one's life is well underway by the time one reaches retirement. For many older adults, this story forms the basis of the identity that will assist them to negotiate the significant losses of growing old: loss of physical and mental capacities, loss of significant others, loss of meaningful work, loss of significance in a child-oriented culture, and loss of income. Yet, with a well-established faith story, elders can find increased possibilities for life fulfillment.

Life review is a natural process used by elders to bring nurture to their lives in the present. Life review is characterized by the elders returning to past events and reliving them in the present through memory. Pastoral care involves assisting this process of life review so that the elder discerns God's story at work in the memory. I find delight when I talk with our aging church members on my pastoral visits. They often relate significant stories of their lives in the church. I find my own life enriched by their review, and I feel spiritually blessed when I see God's work in their lives. Not only am I blessed as I hear their stories unfold, but they also are blessed, in that their living memories include continued sustenance in God's unfolding story. My role as a pastor is to listen and rejoice.

Older people sometimes bring out pictures as they review their lives, and I encourage them to show the pictures and tell stories related to them. This is a good way to encourage life review; pastoral care through the use of pictures helps aging persons to recover significant memories.

On one occasion I visited an elder who had lost her son about twenty years earlier. The anniversary of his death was near, and she was depressed. I noticed pictures of her son on the mantle, and I asked her to tell me about them. She gently picked up a picture and shed a few tears. Then she began to relate a story about the time the picture was made. The picture reminded her of a time when her son was with her and of the meaningful moments they had together. This recalling of past events enabled her to balance the sad feelings with positive memories. The very act of sharing a story about the picture helped her come out of her depression.

Sometimes older people have painful memories or concerns about broken relationships with children or significant others. In such instances, stories are not nurturing devices but instead cause problems to linger. When an elder raises these concerns, pastoral care should involve prayer for hurt memories by asking God, through the power of the Holy Spirit, to make it possible for past relationships to be healed. I often ask God to reveal to an elder how God is working to heal broken relationships. I ask also that the elder be given the wisdom and power to respond to what God is doing to heal past hurts. The goal is to help the elder cooperate with what God is doing to assist in the life-review process. The assumption is that God is at work in the life-review process to bring healing and wholeness.

The Role of the Pastor as Caregiver in Life Crises

This chapter has explored a narrative approach to selected life crises. The emphasis has been on predictable crises that people encounter throughout life. The role of the pastor has been described as helping those in crises understand what they are experiencing, facilitating the expression of feelings, and helping individuals mobilize resources for responding to the crisis. Narrative is a helpful resource for both the pastor and lay caregiver. As caregivers, the pastor and layperson attend to the person's story and find ways to influence the crisis by sharing stories from their own life experiences. Moreover, the caregiver functions to help those in crisis discern and attend to the faith story at work in their lives.

This new edition introduced the re-parenting phenomenon. We can no longer assume that African Americans have the advantage of cross-generational connections that fostered positive internalization that provided internal care and nurture and emotional resources. Thus, contemporary persons transitioning through the life cycle are more vulnerable during these transitions. Yet the vulnerability is not fatal if there are efforts to reconnect and create village functions that sustain people through the life cycle. The liturgical year and the accompanying rituals provide important opportunities for the church to be a nurturing community so that emotional support systems are formed.

CHAPTER FIVE

A NARRATIVE APPROACH TO PREMARRIAGE, MARRIAGE, AND FAMILY COUNSELING

African American pastors have opportunities to do premarriage, marriage, and family counseling. When working with a narrative approach, pastors draw on their own experiences, their experiences of working with others, and the Bible for stories that can help them facilitate wholeness in marriages and in families. This chapter focuses on premarriage counseling as a predictable life transition, and on marriage and family counseling as crises bring changes within the family that call for new patterns of response.

Viewed from a narrative perspective, premarriage counseling is an effort of the engaged couple to fashion a marital narrative out of their own experiences as a couple. "Couple narrative" refers to stories a couple develops, stories that have their roots in the image of the ideal mate that each spouse brings to the marital relationship.[1] During premarriage the couple begins a story history that will be formed through ritualistic rehearsals on a daily basis. "Ritualistic rehearsals" are repetitive activities that form a context for shaping a couple narrative. Taking meals together, attending church, and periodic nights out are examples of ritualistic activities.

Families also have narratives that inform how family members relate. Every family visualizes itself in a particular way. The family has images and themes that influence its behavior. The narrative of the family defines who the family is and how the family behaves. From a narrative perspective, pastoral care to engaged couples, to married couples, and to families focuses on how pastors and laypeople can influence the narrative of couples and families. The emphasis is on caregivers who seek to influence the narrative of couples and families by sharing stories from their own lives and experiences.

PREMARRIAGE, MARRIAGE, AND FAMILY IN THE TWENTY-FIRST CENTURY

Robert Michael Franklin in *Crisis in the Village: Restoring Hope in African American Communities* presents what I consider the most comprehensive analysis of marital and family life in the African American community to date. His analysis of the state of marriage and family life in the past and in the present will set the stage for conversation in the black church for the near and long-term future. This work raises the major questions that African American pastoral care must address. After reviewing a list of eleven dimensions that all should know about African American marriages and families in the United States, he attempts to pose the most central question with which African Americans and the black church must address. He asks the question, *what is wrong?* Then he posits the answer. He says: "I would submit that all of us should be addressing the topic of reviving a culture of healthy relationships and restoring an ethic of commitment in our village."[2] He calls for African Americans and the church to begin a national conversation about healthy relationships. He visualizes healthy relationships as interpersonal bonds that are "characterized by mutuality, trust, respect, nonviolence, and sharing."[3]

It is the reviving of a culture of commitment, and I feel this is the most central point of what Franklin has to say for pastoral care and counseling for the twenty-first century. He concludes that relationships matter, dating matters, ideals and norms matter, expanded understandings of family structure matters, family policy matters, ethics matter, fathers matter, faith matters, violence shatters, and reviving of a culture of commitment matters.[4] Reviving a culture of commitment involves the entire African American community dealing with issues such as dating, the state of marriage, good parenting, domestic violence, sexuality, homosexuality, and same-sex marriage. Despite the devastating impact of slavery and a history of oppression on the culture of commitment, Franklin feels that a case can be made contemporarily for commitment and family life. He believes a case can be made and should be made for the benefits of marital and family life based on his review of the literature. Keeping in mind Franklin's emphasis on the need for establishing a culture of commitment and his making a case for committed marital and family life, I now turn to the task of revising this chapter on premarriage, marriage, and family counseling.

As I reviewed this chapter for the revision, I came to the conclusion that the material contained in this chapter needed very little updating. The need to address reestablishing village functions and the communal nature of storytelling was already present, along with the indigenous storytelling model. There is a need, however, to explore briefly the theological meaning of eschatological narrative practice in relationship to premarriage, marriage, and family. This is particularly the case when we think about the need to establish what Franklin calls a culture of commitment. The chapter already captures how storytelling contributes to the novel ways that marriage and family life can remain resilient and thriving in the twenty-first century. There is need, however, to update the focus of this chapter in light of the culture of commitment, and I will do so by focusing on the concept of eschatological narrative practice. Such an update will reinforce the role of the indigenous storyteller in relationship and in promoting a culture of commitment in premarriage, marriage, and family counseling.

ESCHATOLOGICAL NARRATIVE PRACTICE

Just as the church is an institution formed to carry out the ministry of Jesus Christ through the power of the Holy Spirit, the institutions of marriage and the family can also be instruments that serve the ends of the ministry of Jesus Christ. They can become instruments that mediate God's grace and mercy not only to those who are married and to those within the family but also to those outside the church, because none are beyond the love of God through the power of the Holy Spirit.

The way in which the institutions of marriage and the family engage in eschatological practice is that they serve the ends of drawing those within the marriage and the family into the unfolding eschatological story of God. Those who are married and those within families have encountered God's presence in their relationships, and they have discovered God's divine purpose for their own lives. They have been drawn into God's plan of salvation, and they see very clearly how their married and family lives serve the ends of ministry within and outside the marriage. They not only discern but also embrace what God is doing within them as well as for others through their marriage and family life. In these ways, they recognize that marriage and family can be a call to ministry as well as a vehicle for extending God's grace beyond themselves.

As a calling, marriage and family life become a way of participating in the unfolding of God's story and activity of salvation and liberation. Those within the marriage and family take seriously the need to reflect God's faithfulness to covenantal relationships through the creation of care and nurture for those within the family as well as extending such care and nurture to those beyond the marital and family boundaries. Moreover, marriages and families that embrace the calling to participate in God's unfolding drama of salvation also become examples for others of what is possible for them in marital and family life.

Understanding marriage and family life as a calling may be an important means for African American Christians to help restore a culture of commitment. What is striking to me is that Robert Franklin talks about how the culture of commitment toward marriage and family life was sustained during and after slavery in the midst of oppression. Franklin points out: "Despite the frequent breakup of black families on plantations, many fathers and mothers succeeded in maintaining lasting relationships."[5] He continues: "Marriage and family love survived against all the odds." Indeed, concluding that this was heroic bonding and commitment in tragic circumstances is appropriate.[6]

The key is that the source of such commitment was religious values. This was consistently the case during post-slavery when religious values were drawn on to restore the fractured family torn apart by slavery.[7] Thus, a case can be made for seeing marriage and family life as a calling understood as one means of being faithful to how God uses us in drawing others into God's salvation drama.

The pivotal dynamic in returning to a culture of commitment is the reality that commitment has to be caught more than taught. The conversations that Franklin talks about in his book are extremely important, but these conversations need to include the notion that commitment grows out of couples and families experiencing commitment in their own lives from birth to death. Theologically, commitment comes as one experiences God's faithful commitment to us as human beings. For example, Enoch Oglesby in a new book entitled *Pressing Toward the Mark: Christian Ethics for the Black Church Today* focuses on the importance of faith in ethics among African Americans, especially in the lives of people like Mary McLeod Bethune, Coretta Scott King, and Rosa Parks.[8] For him, faith is trusting God to lead and guide us toward the right thing to do in social situations.[9] The key is that this must be experienced as we live out our married and family lives experiencing God's presence in our relationships as well as God guiding us toward God's ends.

From an eschatological practice point of view, pastoral care and counseling practice is helping couples and families identify God's presence in their lives drawing them toward commitment to their marital partners as well as to the calling that emerges out of being committed to each other and to discerning God's leadership in marriage. Faith emerges when couples have learned to rely on God to lead them, and it emerges when families learn to trust God to guide them.

Theologically, the problem facing the culture of commitment today is that the modern attitude is distrust of God's providence, as Charles Gerkin says in one of the most significant books written on pastoral care in the twentieth century, *Crisis Experience in Modern Life: Theory and Theology for Pastoral Care*.[10] The key experience of modern people is the loss of trust in God's participation in our lives and in guiding us toward important purposes and ends.

My experience in pastoral care and counseling is that part of our task is to help people learn to trust God's presence in our relationships and to recover what premodern Christian thinkers practiced prior to the Enlightenment, which began the modern period of distrust of God, the church, and its leadership. A culture of commitment is built in each marriage and family when, through the eschatological practice of leaders of the family, the couple learns to trust God's presence and activity in their relationships. This trust leads them toward enhanced marital and family relationships as well as toward a calling to a significant service outside the marriage and family.

Trusting God's presence within marital and family relationships as the foundation for restoring the culture of commitment has been demonstrated time and time again in the lives of people with whom I have counseled as well as from those with whom I have come in contact. I am thinking of a crack addict, who found God working on his behalf in his marriage, and I watched and supported him through counseling as God led him through the recovery from drug addiction back into a marriage and family life of commitment. I have also watched a husband who, after many years of an affair, recognized that God was leading him to break a family's generational legacy of infidelity and neglect of the spouse. I also am aware of men who recognized that the marriage they were in would not work, but they found

God leading them to become more responsible parents to their children despite their divorces.

The phrase "God is faithful" is significant, and God's faithfulness is the key factor in helping couples and family members discover their commitment to relationships.

PREMARRIAGE

Premarriage counseling presents the pastor with an opportunity to explore the personal stories that people bring to marriage. Each person brings images of the ideal mate; each person also brings expectations about parents, in-laws, and siblings. They have expectations regarding adjusting to new friends and relating to old friends. There are also concerns about religious activities and other outside activities. In premarriage counseling from a narrative perspective, the pastor is concerned about the story that each person brings, and in what way the personal stories may affect the couple's relationship.

A major concern of black couples who are considering marriage is that they will leave their families of birth and form a couple narrative. The basic concern is that loyalty will be transferred from one's family-of-origin narrative to a new narrative, a couple narrative. The following approach to premarriage counseling illustrates how one pastor sought to prepare engaged couples for that transition. I am indebted to my own father for this point of view; he often talked about what he did in premarriage counseling.

1. The first question I ask a couple before they get married is, *What is the foundation of a happy and enduring home?* Of course, some of them come to it almost immediately, and some beat around the bush and never quite answer the question. Some say getting along with each other. Finally, if they do not get it themselves, I tell them.

2. I tell them that the foundation of a happy and enduring marriage is love and loyalty. When things go haywire, then there is something in love and loyalty to fall back on. If they build their marriage on

financial considerations alone, for example, there is nothing to support the marriage when the couple suffers hard times.

3. The next question I ask is, *Where is your loyalty?* In my own pastoral experience, this is where a marriage has its difficulty. Many couples don't know their first loyalty. Some of them say their first loyalty is to their mother. If they are not able to answer the question, I tell them that their first loyalty is to each other, and that they should not let their mothers, fathers, sisters, or brothers come between them as husband and wife. As a couple, they no longer will be two individuals; rather, they will become one. I warn them that their relatives and friends will interfere, and that they must be very sure that their loyalty is to each other.

4. Then I ask them about their finances and find out the kind of living arrangements they are making, whether they will be living with their parents. I then explain to them the dangers of such an arrangement, similar to the dangers to young adults from parents and relatives. I tell them it is best to get their own quarters, separate from their parents and relatives, if possible.

5. I try to find out if the couple is aware of the conflicts they will have in marriage. I ask them where they will turn if they have a problem that lasts more than a week, which they cannot solve by sitting down in conversation. Many of them say that they will turn to friends and parents for advice. I warn them that this often causes more harm than good, because parents and relatives take sides. I tell them they need to seek outside help—a pastor who is trained in marriage counseling or a professional counselor. Trained counselors lead you to find your own answers to problems and do not give the wrong (unprofessional) advice.

I have developed this approach to premarriage counseling from my own experience. I have dealt with interference in my own marriage from my relatives, and I have counseled many couples who have had this problem. The biblical reference to couples cleaving to each other and the marriage ritual of my own denomination have been very helpful to me in this area.

Narrative Reflection

My father once explained to me how he formulated his approach to premarriage counseling. He pointed out the role played by his own experience, as well as his understanding of the Bible and the marriage ritual. His experience and his methods for solving his own difficulties with relatives became the basic sources of his pastoral care, and the Bible and the marriage service gave normative support.

In black pastoral care, it was customary to draw upon personal experience and biblical tradition. That is, my father had no behavioral models to draw upon that were adequate for his needs. His approach is illustrative of inductive guidance in historical pastoral care. "Inductive" pastoral care refers to drawing upon the pastor's and parishioners' own experiences.

My dad was not addressing the narratives of couples directly; rather, he used his own experiences to develop a series of questions to ask engaged couples. These questions, however, served to reveal the nature of the personal narrative that each person brought to the marriage. I have often heard my dad say that many soon-to-be-married couples brought to marriage a story that had as its foundation primary loyalty to one's family of birth. He indicated he knew that this would lead to marital conflict, so he sought to address primary loyalties right away. Not only would he use his own struggles in early marriage as an example, but he would bring into the counseling biblical references to leaving mother and father and cleaving only to one's own mate. In this way he was seeking to lay the groundwork for the man and woman to fashion a new couple narrative.

From the point of view of premarriage and eschatological narrative practice, my father was also utilizing his own understanding of faith and his own experience of marriage and family life to draw others into an understanding that laid the foundation for the couple to also become a vehicle for mediating God's grace through their relationship. Encountering premarital counseling within the context of congregational life exposes the couple not only to the pastor's wise counsel but also to how the minister lives out his or her own marital and family life. Being positive examples of marital and family life within the life of the congregation reinforces pre-marital counseling.

MARRIAGE

Pastoral care to couples during crisis relates to the way the couple narrative sustains and nurtures the couple in times of difficulty. When a couple faces obstacles that cannot be resolved through the customary resources, the pastor's role is to help them bring their couple narrative to bear on the crisis. Sometimes the narrative is adequate, and sometimes it is not, so the role of the pastor is to assess the narrative and its potential use in crisis. If the couple narrative is adequate and capable of sustaining the couple, the pastor facilitates its use; if it is inadequate, the pastor must help the couple to edit it.

As previously indicated, a couple narrative is a story that a married couple fashion together, a story rooted in the image of the ideal spouse that each spouse brings to the marriage. A healthy couple narrative is one that the couple has revised so that each spouse's ideal-spouse image is based upon a realistic image of the actual spouse. This more realistic narrative recognizes the strengths and weaknesses of each spouse, so that each acts with the other in realistic ways. The unhealthy couple narrative is one in which either one or both spouses maintain the ideal-spouse image, in spite of the realistic nature of the spouses; this narrative supports unrealistic behavior toward one or both spouses that is frustrating and destructive.

One of the primary couple narratives relates to the way a couple handles differentness. Differentness is rooted in the fact that each person in a marital relationship is different and unique. A healthy couple narrative is rooted in the realization that the spouses are different, and the narrative supports each spouse's differentness. An unhealthy narrative ignores that differentness and seeks to force each spouse into the other's ideal-spouse image, without regard for the uniqueness or differentness of the actual spouse. The role of the caregiver is to help the couple with a healthy narrative to bring it to bear on a crisis. When the couple has an unhealthy narrative, the goal of the caregivers is to help them edit this narrative by enabling each spouse to accept the differentness of the other.

The following example of a healthy couple narrative is based on the realization that two people do not need to be in agreement to have a good marital relationship. This couple's ability to resolve crises within their relationship was rooted in their view of themselves as a couple and in the way they were able to accept their personal differences. Their need was to realize that each spouse had a different religious disposition. Each was raised in a different denomination and had different levels of comfort in terms of worship preference. One spouse was Baptist and preferred informal and spontaneous worship with emotional expressiveness. The other spouse was raised in an Episcopal tradition and preferred more form with less spontaneity. They had experimented for a long time and found that they could not find a happy medium. A crisis developed when the couple realized that they could not comfortably modify their personal orientations. They felt that this differentness would lead to a marital split, since both had believed "a family that worships together, stays together."

The pastor who intervened discovered that they had developed a couple-worship style of prayer, song, and Bible reading. They did this daily and found it very satisfying. The pastor supported their private family worship as appropriate and told them that this qualified as the kind of worship that met their beliefs. The pastor also indicated that the storied life they would develop in private couple worship could sustain them, despite their preference for different types of public worship. The pastor also shared several stories of successful couples who, because of personal preferences, attended different churches throughout their married life. The pastor emphasized, however, that couple private worship rituals were important to foster because of their apparent differentness and preferences.

The pastor was able to use a constructive couple narrative history of worship, as well as several stories from his own experience, to help the couple resolve their difficulty. However, not every couple in crisis has a storied history of supporting spousal differentness. In fact, some couples cannot resolve a crisis because of the inability to accept individual differences.

I am reminded of a couple in which the husband had a particular preference in terms of homemaking. During courtship, his wife-to-be raised no real opposition to his expectations. Both were college graduates, but the husband expected his wife to suppress her career and professional goals. After a year of marriage the wife's career goals surfaced. At first the husband ignored them, and when his wife quietly persisted, a crisis developed. The husband's ideal image of a wife was challenged. He made several unsuccessful efforts to force his wife to conform to his expected ideal image. He would not support her career goals and would reinforce only behavior that related to the traditional role of the housewife. When this lack of support became unbearable, the couple went to the pastor. The husband expected the pastor to reinforce a particular biblical view of the husband as the head of the household and the wife as helpmate; the wife hoped the pastor would remain more open and help them work through the crisis.

The pastor realized the crisis was one of differentness. Apparently, both had an implied or implicit agreement about marital roles, but after marriage the wife no longer was happy with the contract. She felt the contract was detrimental and she wanted to renegotiate. Because the pastor recognized the need to respect the wife's emerging professional career identity and the husband's need to accept his wife's emerging sense of self, he began to explore a biblical image of mutuality because of the couple's rootedness in a biblical understanding of marriage.

Using Ephesians 5:21-33, the pastor emphasized verses 21, 25, and 28, indicating that this was a passage of mutuality, where the true head of the house was one who created an environment where all family members could grow. The husband found the passage interesting, but he was reluctant to buy into the pastor's interpretation.

The pastor realized that the crisis would not be resolved immediately and began to lay the foundation for helping the couple move toward a narrative history that included acceptance of differences. He told a story about a husband and wife who accepted a biblical interpretation of non-mutual family headship, pointing out that this interpretation remained dominant for years, until one day the couple discovered that they had grown into mutuality. After telling this story, the pastor asked the couple to reflect on it while they set aside several sessions to discuss the marital crisis.

By using a Bible passage as well as a story from his own experience, the pastor helped the couple begin to edit their own narrative. The pastor understood the psychological principle of differentness, as well as the theological principle of mutuality in marital relationships, and he used these principles in a narrative model to help the couple in their crisis.

FAMILY

Crisis in family life occurs when the family as a whole faces obstacles that cannot be resolved with its ordinary methods of problem solving. Normally, families have patterns that help the members function. Husbands and wives find ways to respond to each other; parents find ways to raise children; and children find ways to relate to their parents and to one another. Whether these ways of relating are healthy or unhealthy, the family rarely questions these patterns until a crisis develops. Then the customary patterns are challenged, and the family seeks to recover these patterns as much as possible.

Often a family turns to its pastor when there is a crisis and they need help to restore the family to its former customary functioning. Then the pastor must assess whether the family is living a healthy story and determine how to use the family story, if it is healthy, as a resource in resolving the crisis; or the pastor must help the family edit its unhealthy story.

A healthy family has a realistic story that will help it respond to a crisis. An unhealthy family has a story that designates someone within the family to blame for the crisis, which results in a faulty crisis resolution. In other words, a healthy family story enables the family to face the problem head-on and support each family member emotionally during the crisis, but an unhealthy family story designates one family member as the cause of the problem. The end result is that the rest of the family lives at the expense of another family member.

The role of the caregiver in counseling a family with a healthy story is to enable that story to sustain the family until the crisis is resolved. An example of such a family story is one in which the members genuinely care for one another and reinforce their emotional ties when facing obstacles. The role of the pastor is to help family members care for one another as they face the crisis. A healthy family scenario is one that says, "We can handle anything as long as we stick together and continue to care for one another." I heard of one such family in which the father was laid off because of cutbacks at the factory. Fortunately, he received some severance and vacation pay and also was eligible for unemployment compensation. All the family members sat down and looked at the family financial needs and discovered they could make it for about three months before they felt a real financial crunch.

The pastor visited the family to see if they needed help. The whole family, including two children and the husband's mother, welcomed the pastor. When the pastor indicated that he was especially concerned about the family's financial and emotional strength, he discovered they had already made survival plans that included a slight modification in spending and the postponement of purchases until they were financially able. The children knew that things would be hard, that they would not have money for things that were not essential. The husband admitted that at first he had been really worried, but when he had faced the family with the reality, the members had responded that they had weathered worse storms in the past, and they felt they had the resources to handle this crisis.

After listening to their story and how they had marshaled their resources as a family, the pastor affirmed the positive family story and told them about how the early church had surrounded Peter with prayer when he was arrested. He indicated that the entire church would be praying for the family, just as it had prayed for Peter. When the pastor left, he knew this family was facing its crisis with a positive story; they had the necessary resources to face the problem and resolve it. His role was to reinforce the existing resources and to use the faith story to reinforce the positive family resources. He wanted to communicate to the family that God's story also was sustaining them and that they had support from a caring congregation.

Sometimes families with negative stories will label one family member as the cause of a family problem. The role of the pastor in such a situation is to help the family modify its negative story so that it can better resolve the crisis. The pastor can tell stories that help the family face the problems head-on, rather than designate one member as the cause. The following example illustrates this well.

The family (which we will call the Jones family, consisting of Esther, age 30; George, 34; and four children: two boys, ages 6 and 8; two girls, ages 9 and 11) still lived in a small apartment in the home of George's mother at the time of the intervention. Esther and George had been married eleven years. Esther was a housewife, and George worked for the city and also was in partnership with several friends in a clothing store. His pay was barely enough to make ends meet.

George was extremely close to his mother and was inclined to accept her advice rather than his wife's concerning the needs of the children. Being the landlady, George's mother felt that she had the right to enter the Jones home whenever she deemed it necessary, and her intrusions formed the basis for constantly recurring fights between George and Esther. The involvement of Esther's family was evidenced by the fact that her four brothers and sisters often cared for the children when Esther needed to rest. Violent arguments erupted among all family members. Esther went to the pastor, complaining that she feared George had become involved with another woman. The pastor had observed the great deal of tension that existed in the family and was glad Esther was seeking aid. After he listened to Esther's story, he decided he needed to talk to the husband before trying to determine the cause of the problem. When he visited the home and talked to the husband, to each child, and to the mother-in-law, the pastor discovered that the children became involved in the marital arguments. Their story was that they were concerned that their father might become violent with their mother, although they felt that their mother was too nagging and should back off. They also told him that they would intervene to try to lessen the loud shouting and bring some degree of reason to the situation.

When the pastor realized that this was a true family crisis that would require long-term counseling and that he did not have the time or the skill to take on the problem, he approached the family about referring them to a family counselor. There was a great deal of resistance from both George and Esther. George believed the problem was Esther's fault; he felt she didn't know how to raise children or make a home inviting for a man. Esther believed the problem was George's fault; she felt he was a mama's boy who let his mother make all the decisions. Each felt that family counseling would be of no value because the problem was the other spouse's problem.

The pastor's goal became one of preparing the couple for referral to family counseling. The pastor felt that several sessions were necessary for the family to realize that there were serious problems within the family that could not be blamed on any one individual. The pastor decided that both George and Esther must get beyond blaming the other if they were to focus on the real problem, which was that they had not developed their own relationship as husband and wife. Rather, they had allowed unnecessary intrusions from their children and from George's mother to affect their relationship and the raising of their children.

The pastor sought to lay the groundwork by telling a story from his own life. He told the couple about a problem his daughter once had in school. He said that he and his wife had blamed each other for the problem, with charges and countercharges. Then one day, the daughter had shouted that both of them were the problem, because they never could come to any common understanding about anything. The pastor used negative narratives to edit and revise their narratives. The goal of such storytelling is to enable the couple or family to face the crisis and resolve it.

MARRIAGE AS A CALLING

Frankly, it was not until revising this book that I began to think about marriage as a calling. I have had one notable case where a couple having severe marital problems found healing because they found a sense of calling in the midst of their problems. I will bring this chapter to a close by focusing on how a sense of calling informed how a married couple discovered God at work in their marriage and family life and drew on it to come to grips with some very serious personal and marital problems.

Greg and Judy had been married for ten years. Judy originally came to counseling because she had a drinking problem and often used cocaine recreationally. She came for personal counseling realizing that the problem had gotten out of hand and was affecting her marriage and the raising of her two children.

Greg and Judy are African Americans in their mid-thirties. Greg is a very successful health care practitioner. Judy was bored at home and sought to flee the boredom through the use of cocaine and alcohol. Her parents were nearby and they would take the children at times while she was taking her drugs at home. In counseling Judy said that she wanted to overcome her problem.

Not long into the counseling, she began to complain about her husband treating her like a child and how he was trying to confiscate her drugs and alcohol. When the concern in counseling became her husband, I asked her to invite him into our sessions, which she did. From the very beginning he was very cooperative and wanted to be very cooperative. He admitted his concern for his wife and her abuse of two substances.

He immediately recognized that he was a codependent in that he participated in enabling her substance abuse through his behavior. He was a child of an alcoholic father who was completely irresponsible, and he had reversed roles with his father. He would often have to go find his father and bring him home after one of his binges.

Greg saw the connection between his father and his wife and how there was an emotional way in which he enabled his wife. Thus, the counseling began to focus more on Greg while Judy listened. One day, Greg brought out the fact that he was a religious person, and he did not want to live his life the way he had in the past. He said he had a lot of guilt because he had been engaging in a long-term affair outside of his marriage. He wanted it to stop. He saw himself like his father, and he felt that he needed to end the generational curse so it would not be carried on in the life of his three-year-old son. He said he felt strongly the leading of God to come to grips with his own problems, and he knew that he had to go through some very hard times in his marital relationship before things would get better. He said he was committed to his marriage, and he would do whatever it took.

Judy felt completely betrayed by his infidelity. Her rage toward him was deep, and she lashed out at him with tirades that were uncontrollable. Sometimes Judy would express her deep rage at him in counseling, which made me uncomfortable. When I asked Greg how he felt about her raging outburst, he said he had it coming. He said he saw this as important for her recovery and for their relationship. He said he was in the marriage to stay for the sake of everybody, and he would do what he had to do.

Judy and Greg went to different churches. Judy found a religiously conservative church to attend because she had a prayer partner there who was like a grandmother to her. She found unconditional positive regard in this relationship. This was a very positive relationship, and this helped her gradually drink less and less and give up cocaine altogether. Greg joined her at church and continued to come to counseling. After many months Judy finally got over her rage, and it was possible for them to repair the damage in their relationship. Greg gave up the affair very early, and it seemed as though Judy's rage lessened when she came to realize that Greg was truly committed to her and to being a better husband and father.

I know that God's presence working in Greg and Judy and in their re-lationship was the central factor in the healing of their relationship. Every now and then I hear from them, and after six years, they are doing fine. The narrative feature in their relationship had to do with Greg's family legacy of addiction and his understanding of the Bible and generational curses. He would often use his reading of the Bible and his understanding of breaking generational curses to help him change. Judy used her prayer partner and regular church attendance to help her in her recovery as well. It was both of their responses to God's presence and their trusting in God's guidance to lead them out of their difficulty.

The village has collapsed. But God is leading us to recover many vil-lage functions. The eschatological narrative practice of trusting God's lead-ing and God's unfolding story of restoring village functions helps sustain and build vital marriages and families.

CHAPTER SIX

PASTORAL CARE AND HUMAN SEXUALITY

Addressing premarriage, marriage, and family relationships without addressing human sexuality is a serious error when facing the twenty-first century. Thus, a new chapter is added to this book with the intent of helping those in pastoral care help people struggle with what will continue to be a major problem. This chapter explores the complex nature of human sexuality and provides some windows for approaching it within the context of African American churches. There is urgency because of HIV/AIDS and the public discussion about sexual diversity, especially the concern over homosexuality and same-sex marriage. It would be irresponsible for pastoral care and counseling practitioners to avoid the subject of human sexuality. This chapter recognizes also that there are a variety of voices on human sexuality among African Americans and that it is important to understand this diversity.

THE FORMATION OF HUMAN SEXUALITY

Pastoral care is always about conversations in which people engage, and it is absolutely imperative to understand how these conversations shape our understanding of human sexuality. The goal of pastoral care is to construct an open and safe environment in order for people to examine and explore the many conversations that are taking place today about human sexuality. This is crucial because there are a variety of conversations about human sexuality, and how we internalize conversations about human sexuality is crucial for our health and well-being.

I will draw on my own experience as a pastoral counselor working with people concerning sexual issues for forty years. My perspective is only one perspective, but the value of it is that I have had the privilege of watching people sift through many such conversations until they finally come to their own voice about what they really believe about the place of sex in their lives.

First, sexuality is more than the act of sexual intercourse. Human sexuality is about biology, yes; but it is also about complex relationships and meanings that we bring to all human relations as well as how we communicate with others. My appreciation of the complexity of human sexuality has come primarily from women with whom I have worked over the years, and I have come to the conclusion that men and women are not much different when it comes to emotions and interpersonal relationships. We are human beings, and we are influenced deeply by all the dimensions of all our relationships.

Second, there is no such thing as casual sex. There is no such thing as a one-night stand. The act of sexual intercourse is a delicate process of human communication where we internalize another person to the point that this person becomes part of our lives. This is true for both males and females.

What then is human sexuality? Sexuality is about a relational wholeness in which mind, body, spirit, and relationships with others are interconnected in mutually interactive ways. "Sexuality is integral to biological, psychological, and spiritual wholeness. Personal identity and the ego itself are distinctly sexual."[1] African Americans have understood black sexuality to be integral to all of life, including spirituality, relationships, and physical expressions.[2]

Learning about sexuality is shaped by private and public conversations within families, in close relationships with others, and through wider cultural understandings.[3] The key to learning about sexuality in black congregations is both doctrinal and behavioral. Doctrinal conversations about sexuality in African American churches are consistently conservative and orthodox, staying within the tradition of Greco-Roman dualism, where there is alienation between the body and the spirit.[4] Drawing on Greco-Roman dualism, African American Christian orthodoxy confines sexual intercourse to heterosexual marital relationships. Yet, at the behavioral level there is a silent tolerance of a great diversity of sexual practices including extramarital affairs, homosexuality, and same-sex relationships.[5] Robert Franklin attributes this quiet tolerance concerning sexual practices, including gay and lesbian relationships, to an ethic of family pluralism and folk wisdom.[6] He says that this ethic has eroded recently due to anxiety by Christians that the normative status of traditional heterosexuality within black sexuality is being lost. Theologically, Franklin is concerned with restoring reconciliation within the black community where a village renewal process takes place, rooted in a spiritual process where transformed lives are the result.[7]

Like Franklin, I am concerned with renewal of village processes. My own way of talking about village renewal is through the concept of narrative pastoral conversation, and I compare a propositional conversation with a narrative-oriented conversation. "The narrative oriented conversation is contrasted with the propositional conversational orientation, and narrative pastoral care in sexual diversity attempts to create a caring environment in which all God's children are envisaged as vital members of God's family and are treated as family members, rather than outsiders."[8] Conservative approaches to sexuality use the propositional rule of law and use exclusion from community to force those who do not adhere to the heterosexual norms out of the community. The narrative orientation, however, focuses on inclusion of all persons in the village regardless of sexual orientation or sexual practice so that no one is excluded from the transforming power of the unfolding story of God.[9]

The narrative orientation to human sexuality is not anxious about losing the heterosexual norm within the congregation or village life because there is something deeper going on within the life of the congregation and village. What is going on relates to being touched by the presence of God in congregational life. Rudy Rasmus in *Touch: The Power of Touch in Transforming Lives* says that he often got questions in his growing congregation: "What are we going to do with all these gays and lesbians (or addicts or mentally ill persons or gang members or homeless people or whoever) who come to church here?"[10] He concludes that inquisitions within congregations are rooted in value judgments based on outward appearances without intimate knowledge and touching of people in meaningful ways. He said he fought with boldness to make sure all persons were included so that they could feel touched by God and experience a taste of the love that permeated the church. Authentic love transforms people's lives.

The point is that learning about human sexuality must take place in an atmosphere of love and care where people can bring who they are without fear of being excluded. Within a caring community people can work through all the conversations that they have heard in their lives and make up their own minds about how they will live out their sexuality. Anxiety about loss of the heterosexual norm lessens since it is God's transforming love that has an impact on all of our lives.

THE CLINICAL MODEL OF PASTORAL CARE

The narrative model of pastoral care of human sexuality developed out of my own clinical experience and practice over forty years. Pastoral care relies on the clinical model in that it is concerned with how human beings attribute meaning to their experience. From the perspective of the clinical model, the meaning of human sexuality emerges within the context of the relationship between the pastoral caregiver and the person needing care.

I have found that certain counselees present a clearer picture of how the meaning of human sexuality emerges than others. I call such cases signature cases in that they point to unique ways of understanding the function of sexuality in the contemporary world. There are persons with tremendous introspective insight and ability who provide perspectives and create clear pictures of how to bring meaning to our contemporary sexual lives. Moreover, the experience of the pastoral caregiver in the clinical model also contributes to helping people express the meanings that they generate in the pastoral counseling conversation. The implication for this chapter is that there will be key counselees whose lives are excellent examples for helping us visualize how we come to understand ourselves as sexual beings.

One key question that this chapter seeks to answer is *how do sexual intercourse and genital sexual relief function in our contemporary society?* In our culture where the village has broken down and people cannot rely on crossgenerational relationships for human validation of their worth as they once did, sexual intercourse takes on increased significance. For example, David Schnarch, a family therapist and sex therapist who draws on the clinical model, indicates that sex, and especially sexual intercourse, becomes a quest for a sense of feeling worthwhile and a sense of self-validation.[11]

Freudian psychology, Self Psychology, and Object Relations theory are modern developments in response to the loss of community. Freudian psychology depended on an intact and repressive society where sexual feelings were denied and guilt over human sexuality was the dominant factor. In the Freudian culture of the late nineteenth and well into the twentieth centuries, abusive parenting was a dominant phenomenon. With Self Psychology, as articulated by Heinz Kohut, and Object Relations theory there was a shift from an emphasis on guilt to one of shame. These theories address the loss of community, and the emotional context of this loss is the feeling of being abandoned by parents. Within this context of abandonment, the need of children is for adequate parenting figure internalization. Thus, the dominant need expressed in shame psychology and Self Psychology is the need for adequate caring parental figures to internalize so that the self can form normally. Lack of such potential internalized parenting figures results in the feeling of being unloved as well as the feeling of never being loved. It is this lack of sufficient parenting figures to internalize that shapes our experience of sex and sexual intercourse in contemporary society.[12] The end result is a quest for adequate loving people to internalize so that self-formation is facilitated.

I have concluded that we live in a shame-oriented society. The striving for adequate internalized relationships makes us vulnerable to exploitation and being used. It opens us up to pursuing any kind of love relationship that holds out the possibility of our being loved.

> I defined shame as feeling unlovable, that one's life has a basic flaw in it. I tried to describe how we live in a shame-prone society in which fulfillment of our need to feel loved and cared for is rapidly disappearing; we begin to settle for any kind of relationships with significant others in which we experience some semblance of nurture and care without having to turn ourselves inside out, in ways that only increase our shame, in order to meet others' expectations. I emphasized that the Spirit of God works on our behalf to help us view ourselves as worthwhile; God also tries to lead us toward the kinds of relationships that help us see ourselves as valuable.[13]

Schnarch talks about the quest in terms of the capacity for self-validated intimacy.[14] For him, the capacity for self-validation rests in self-differentiation, or the ability to be a self apart from others. The self-differentiated person already has an internalized sense of self-worth and validation due to adequately internalized affirming of others. Such people do not need sex or sexual intercourse for self-affirmation. Rather, sex is not a quest for self-worth, but it becomes an expression of one's inner self. Thus, Schnarch develops a concept of self-validated intimacy to express the appropriate place of sexual intercourse in human relationships. He says, "Intimacy is the ability to display one's inner life in relationships with one's partner."[15] Self-validated people do not need sex for self-validation. They are capable of other-validation because they come to sexual relationships with a solid sense of self.

The function of sex, then, is not to affirm our worth and value. Nor is it for increasing intimacy. Rather, it is for expressing the intimacy already existing in our inner lives. Thus, the capacity for sexual intercourse and intimacy takes considerable self-development and interpersonal maturity. The quest for worth and value through sex and sexual intercourse complicates the quest for self-validation.

It is my experience as a pastoral counselor in my clinical practice that sex has become a substitute for relationships, and this substitution results from the loss of village life. Sex functions like a drug of choice for many of us because we think that sex will provide us with the worth and value we seek. In fact, our entire consumer marketing strategy is oriented toward the quest for worth and value through artificial and material means. Modern addictions are a quest for adequate internalized relationships gone amok. That is, we are recruited by our marketing culture into thinking that relationships can never satisfy our need for self-esteem, and only material goods and sex can provide us what we need.

SIGNATURE CLINICAL CASES

Earlier in this chapter I talked about signature clinical cases as prime examples of how sex and sexual intercourse function in today's society. I want to lift up two such cases taken from my own clinical work.

Case I

Karen came for counseling when she was a senior in college. She presented a problem associated with having been celibate for over a year. She felt the need to return to a life of promiscuous sex in order to support herself in the last year of college. She lost her job and her school fees were due. She found work as a waitress at a club. It was known for the waitstaff's sexual encounters with paying customers. She was anxious about her need for money, but she really did not want to return to her former lifestyle.

She felt she could not depend on her parents for help. Her mother had very little money to support herself. She was alienated from her father, and to take money from him had too many strings attached. In fact, she said it would be less abusive to work at the nightclub.

From a faith perspective, Karen was struggling with a call to ministry. She was raised Pentecostal, and she understood all the rules and regulations about sex outside of marriage. She found, however, that people in leadership in her church were not following the rules they espoused. Therefore, she learned that it was possible to separate one's sex life from one's professed beliefs.

She began her sexual experiences very early as a teenager. She learned that there was a great deal of attention paid to her because of her body. She found that she needed the attention from others, and in fact she said she was dependent on that attention. Without the sex, she did not feel she would get the attention. In college, she found that she could make money from sex, and she did so at times by working in sex clubs.

She was promiscuous until she entered her junior year in college. At that time, she felt a calling from God on her life. She took it seriously, and she decided to abstain from sex altogether. She said she became celibate. When she came for counseling, it was late in her junior year of college. Her dilemma as already indicated was whether she would return to her sexual life still of the past in order to have the funds to complete her college education.

A problem surfaced that Karen was not prepared to deal with, although I have heard this same story from many. She had been celibate for over a year. She described what happened to her during the time of her abstinence:

> She said it was a time of purging from her life all the different personalities with whom she had slept. She said that the persons with whom she had slept became part of her, and the celibacy enabled her to extricate them from her life. She did not want to return to a life of promiscuity, because the purging process was extremely painful. To return to her old life would mean a severe setback in her spiritual and emotional growth in her mind. Consequently, she decided to seek counseling so that she could

have emotional and spiritual guidance as she went through a severe crisis in faith. She was feeling called on by a wilderness test similar to the challenge that Jesus had faced with Satan in his early ministry.[16]

This case was a signature one for me in that it provided concrete evidence that no sexual encounters are casual. It reinforced what Masters and Johnson discovered when they trained sexual surrogates as therapists. They had to abandon the practice, realizing that it was too emotionally taxing for the sexual surrogates. Sexual surrogates actually engaged in sexual intercourse with people with sexual problems as a treatment modality.

The case also taught me the wisdom of using the biblical concept of knowing as a way to describe sexual intercourse. More precisely, one meaning of "to know" in the Old Testament relates to sexual intercourse, as in the cases of Genesis 4:1, 17, 25, and Numbers 31:18, 35.[17] Working with this young woman taught me, again, that more goes on in sexual intercourse than we think or imagine.

The case also helped me see the importance of understanding the function of sex and sexual intercourse as the quest for self-validation. Karen never felt affirmed by the sexual encounters. She only felt used. It was only when she developed a personal relationship with God that she felt truly loved and cared for.

In short, as a signature case, Karen's life taught me that sexual intercourse can never be a substitute for real love. Our culture puts too much emphasis on it as a pathway to self-esteem. Sex plays an important role in life, but it will not make us feel good about ourselves when we don't have inner feelings of self-worth. Moreover, sex is never a casual experience; it always means taking into one's self another person. It is not just biological relief.

As a result of Karen's spiritual walk with celibacy, she learned the meaning of 1 Corinthians 6:15-50. Human bodies and spirituality are intricately connected, and what goes on in the body and in the spirit affect each other. She had become one with each of her sexual partners in the sense that they became part of her inner life. She internalized them, and the level of knowledge of the other was profound. It was in no way superficial.

My basic point is that the clinical model helps us envision how people bring meaning to sex. It also helps us test popular meanings that exist in society. The commercial meaning of sex serves the ends of the marketplace, but the clinical model helps us see more deeply into the lives of people and how popular meanings may often distort how complicated sex and sexual intercourse are.

Another signature case for me was a male who also had sex with multiple males. Wayne could be characterized as an emotionally disconnected person.[18] Because he was raised to think he could control his sexual urges, he turned to conservative and fundamental religious beliefs, thinking this could help him. But when he discovered that this did not work either, he came to counseling. He had a compulsive need to become involved with other men sexually, and he expected me to transform his compulsion into something he could control. In fact, he expected me to transform him and eliminate his homosexual compulsions.

My style of pastoral counseling with men who want to overcome their homosexuality is not to agree to enter into this effort. I indicated that I could provide a relationship where Wayne could feel cared for and appreciated. I also told him I would help him to explore his family relationships and how vital they were to him at this point in his life. I also told him I could help him explore his compulsion and how it related to his family of origin, but I told him I would not accept as a goal to change his sexual orientation. He became very angry with me and questioned my role as a minister. Eventually I helped him explore his disappointment in me for not accepting his goal of sexual orientation change. I did, however, help him try to discontinue self-destructive and dangerous behaviors related to promiscuous sexual activity.

I experienced Wayne as a relational refugee who got disconnected from his family of origin and lived almost completely out of his fantasy life. He had no real connections, but somehow his compulsion had something to do with being disconnected. Thus, my counseling goal became to help him connect with me.

What ultimately came across to me was that Wayne did not have the necessary internal validation system in his life. I think he was searching for genuine caring and loving others who he could internalize so that he could have an enduring sense of self. What happened, however, was that Wayne's compulsion kept getting the better of him, but he did use our counseling relationship to some extent to internalize my caring attitude. In fact, we spent many months in counseling. The pattern was that he would leave for several months and later return, then we would begin all over again. Eventually, he left for good. Eventually, he did develop a better relationship with his sister and her children. This was progress.

The clinical method has taught me a lot about sex and sexual intercourse as a means to try to achieve self-validation and worth. A companion method to the clinical model for learning about the quest for self-validation is the use of memoirs, where people tell their own story. One important example of the use of a memoir for charting one's life story and the quest for self-validation is E. Lynn Harris's *What Becomes of the Brokenhearted*.[19] Harris had a long, hard road toward finding self-validation as a gay person. He was a person whose faith in God and relationships with families and friends satisfied his quest for worth and value. He found that God loved him, his family loved him, and his friends loved him. And he found his life's calling in his writing. When visiting a dying friend, he says:

> I realized the world didn't revolve around me and my search for love and self-esteem. I learned that I could face the tough obstacles of seeing someone I loved dying and still maintain my faith in God. I was reminded of the power of family, and the lie that black families were homophobic was dispelled by the love and support every member of Richie's family showed him every day, not because he was dying but because he was their son, husband, brother, uncle, cousin, and friend.[20]

E. Lynn Harris is a signature person whose novels and memoirs help us envision how faith in God and living in community with family and friends are essential to the quest for self-validation. In fact, he says that celibacy and sobriety were essential in helping him make progress toward self-love.[21] He discovered what Karen discovered. That is, he found out that sex or sexual intercourse did not bring healing or help further his quest for self-validation. It was a relationship with God and being part of a loving and caring family and community that, along with a vocation or calling, brought him to self-validation.

THE CHURCH AND HOMOSEXUALITY AND SAME-SEX RELATIONSHIPS

Robert Franklin has put the discussion of homosexuality and same-sex relationships on the church's agenda quite creatively in his *Crisis in the Village*. I want to use his work as a starting point for introducing my own ideas. While he approaches his work as a social ethicist, I will be drawing on the clinical method to address this topic.

Robert Franklin sets forth his views on healthy same-gender relations in the chapter entitled "A Resolution on Faith and Sexuality."[22] He affirms that homosexuals are made in the image of God and deserve love and respect by every community member. There are a diversity of opinions on homosexuality, but we need to be sure that our disagreements do not separate us from the love of God. Homosexuals are here to stay, and we need to find ways to live peaceably together. Homosexuals make significant contributions to our church and society.

Franklin writes that homosexuals who affirm the quality of their relationships are no threat to heterosexual marriages and relationships. Traditional teachings of the black church make it difficult for men to have sex with both men and women. It makes it difficult to be honest about their sexual practices and preferences. He insists that forcing homosexuals to remain in the closet does more damage than good, and it would be better to foster a community of openness. He concludes, "It would be a loving act to enable all adults to be fully and freely who they are before God."[23] He hopes that heterosexual members of communities would help gay, lesbian, bisexual, and transgendered neighbors practice patience as heterosexual members of the church discern and deliberate about homosexual and same-gender relationships. Finally, he would like homosexual members of the community to urge heterosexual community members to respect them as equals and not ask homosexual members to compromise who they are for the sake of heterosexual comfort.

Franklin then goes on to address issues concerning political exploitation of family values; stigmatizing language; state approval of same-sex unions; the inability of the state to legislate what faith determines to be good or right; and the importance of engaging in the process of prayer, discernment, and discussion. He hopes that faith in God will lead us all closer to participating in what God is doing in our midst.

From the clinical perspective, Franklin's resolution is right on. It takes the high road, puts forth the concerns and issues with sensitivity, and urges tolerance on each side. I would, however, also expand his resolution to include formative issues that I consider essential to theological education. The clinical model, taught within the context of theological education, forces students to examine their own views on human sexuality from a critical stance. The goal is to use the theological curriculum and the many diverse theories and perspectives to which the student is exposed, with an eye toward helping the student make theological commitments that are authentic. These commitments include convictions about human sexuality. I believe that students must examine critically the views of human sexuality that they bring to seminary. But they must also have the courage to take a stand when they discover what they truly believe. Their creedal statements should be made recognizing that they are provisional, at best, and that they are grounded in personal beliefs that are not undergirded by the desire to achieve self-validity at the expense of others. Using one's own beliefs and convictions to gain self-validity is a sin. Our self-validity comes from God and not from others. Therefore, our convictions and beliefs about human sexuality must come from our relationship and walk with God.

As a professor of pastoral care, I am obligated to respect what the student decides. Moreover, the student has a right to know about my convictions as well. As professors, we are called to be transparent in the way Robert Franklin demonstrates in his resolution. Therefore, below I will attempt to point out my own convictions, drawing on a chapter entitled "Race and Sex in the Debate over Homosexuality in The United Methodist Church."[24]

I begin my statement about homosexuality and same-sex union with my denominational understanding, which I embrace. I am United Methodist, and I mostly affirm the following theological statements of my denomination. Our *Book of Discipline* states, "Homosexual persons, no less than heterosexual persons, are individuals of sacred worth." While affirming this, it also affirms that homosexual practice is incompatible with Christian teaching, and it prohibits the ordination of practicing homosexuals, forbids clergy blessing or presiding over same-sex unions, and forbids the use of United Methodist facilities for same-sex union ceremonies.[25]

There are several reasons for my support, and I now provide five points of explanation.

1. I was raised in the Methodist Episcopal Church and was a member of this church when licensed to preach and ordained in 1969. This was the denomination in which I was born and in which my parents served. My father served in the denomination for over forty years, and my mother was raised in the Methodist Episcopal Church.

2. My beliefs stem from my original formation community, including my own family of origin. In fact, my parents, and especially my father, were very clear about the subject of homosexuality. His views fit what Robert Franklin calls the ethic of family pluralism, which embodied a folk wisdom that tolerated gay and lesbian members of their families, churches, and villages.[26] More specifically, the

formation of my beliefs and convictions within my family of origin are expressed in my published statements.

My convictions (about homosexuality) stem from the local and contextual theologies I heard growing up as I listened to my parents' stories and sayings. My father was very clear in his feelings about homosexuality, and he was always consistent when we asked him about certain people in our family. He would say that homosexuality was a private affair between God and the person and that the person had to deal with God about his or her own behavior. My father would emphasize that homosexuals are children of God and are recipients of God's grace. Never once did I hear him bash or condemn homosexuals. At the same time, I never heard him endorse the homosexual lifestyle. In general, I believe he and my mother knew that they had to be careful about what they said on the subject of homosexuality because of relatives and friends who were homosexuals. They wanted us to be open. They did not want us to discriminate or be unjust. Our family had endured enough of this, and we did not want to engage in exclusion.[27]

3. When I left Boston University School of Theology after earning three degrees, one of which was a Ph.D. in Pastoral Psychology and Counseling in 1976, I came to Atlanta. I arrived in August of 1975 at the Interdenominational Theological Center very versed in the clinical model. I prided myself for being on the cutting edge of gay and lesbian issues, and I saw myself leading the way in social justice issues related to this topic. In fact, I began supervising one of my students who was an assistant pastor at the Metropolitan Community Church in Atlanta, which welcomed same-sex couples. I helped my male supervisee with his counseling of gay couples. He happened to be white.

While supervising this person, I was also working with African American students who were known to be gay at ITC. In counseling they would tell me about their lifestyle, and I was shocked when they told me not to be too quick to embrace an accepting attitude toward their lifestyle. They indicated that they had tried to embrace this gay lifestyle, and they said that they could not shake their convictions that their gay lifestyle was inconsistent with their spiritual walk with God. I heard this statement time after time. It was at this point that I decided to be more cautious in what I thought about homosexuality.

Of key significance was one gay student with whom I was working. He went for a year-long internship in a city in a well-known African country. He saw himself as bisexual because he had sex with both men and women. I guess he would have been on what we call the "down low." Following his year in Africa he returned home excited, and he could not wait to tell me about the entire year of unintended celibacy. He said he was only interested in sex with men, and he would try every known move he learned in the United States to get men in bed with him. He said they responded to his moves with warmth and friendship, but having genital sex with another male was not part of their experience. Therefore, these men never went there with him. Instead, he found a level of acceptance and friendship, which included touch and hugs. He said he could not wait until he got back to the United States to tell me he found what he had been looking for all his life. He was looking for community and care among men.

It is clear to me that the fear of close and intimate relationships with other males here in the United States is high, and it prevents us from forming the kinds of same-gender relationships that are essential and basic between males and human beings. Of course, I am talking about depth closeness and intimacy without crossing into the genital sexual area. Until males can find genuine companionship with each other without crossing the genital boundary, I think we will never deal with the problems black males face in this country. What I am saying is that there appears to be a major disconnect among black males in the United States, which will not allow us to relate to one another more closely and warmly as males do in other parts of the world. One reason I read the works of E. Lynn Harris is that I think he is on a pilgrimage to teach us how to relate as males to males. He is on a journey, and each one of his books reveals something new about helping men to learn about relating more closely.

4. I support the United Methodist statement on homosexuality because I fundamentally believe that the statement was created out of an understanding of God's grace, both justifying and sanctifying. I believe that it was created out of knowing God's love, and the writers understood that it was not scarce but abundant. Racism, sexism, homophobia, and all "isms" are created based on the theory that grace is scarce because it is a limited commodity; therefore, the access to grace has to be limited. I believe that the framers of our denominational statement on homosexuality believe that certain lifestyles limit the work of grace in people's lives. Moreover, I feel that the desire to keep gays and lesbians within the church reflects the need to make sure that they are not cut off from God's grace. I am aware that God's grace works outside of the established church, where there are "two or three gathered in the name of Jesus." My point is that United Methodist framers of the stand are not functioning out of malice toward gays or lesbians.

5. I also support the United Methodist stand on homosexuality because of a new and different understanding of the flesh. For example, I am excited about what Robert Jewett, a colleague and friend, has just published in his 1140-page commentary on Romans.[28] What excites me is that much of Western theology rests on Pauline writings, and Jewett's scholarship introduces what I consider to be a novel understanding of the flesh that can reshape our understanding of sin in relationship to sex.

Jewett interprets Romans 7:5 in the following way: "For when we were in the flesh, [our] sinful passions that [came] through the law were at work in our members in bearing fruit to death."[29]

Jewett says that we must understand the word *flesh* in light of perverted systems of honor and shame in Paul's time. In fact, he says that flesh had to do less with sensuality than it did to "leading captives into lives of unrelenting competition to gain advantage over other persons and groups."[30] He says that sinful passages about the yearnings of the flesh were more about seeking superior status and rewards in culture, and they did not derive from human sensuality.

Jewett's understanding of flesh is attributed to Paul's pursuit of his own identity and self-worth at the expense of Christians. On the Damascus Road he was competing for personal status and fame through extraordinary obedience to the law. Thus, to be set free from this compulsion to gain honor and fame by meeting the law's demand, he needed Jesus Christ.[31]

My point is that sins of the flesh have a deeper meaning than sensuality, and flesh involves the desire to achieve worth, value, and identity at the expense of some other person or group. Indeed, homophobia, racism, sexism, and all other "isms" are sin precisely because they come at the expense of others. It is my firm belief that The United Methodist Church's stand on homosexuality is not rooted in the flesh or the desire to gain status, honor, fame, reputation, or gain at the expense of gays and lesbians.

There is another concern, however, that needs to be raised. This concern will help bring this chapter to a close. The clinical model has taught me that there are many people who have turned to sex as a method of self-validation. This kind of quest is not at the expense of others; rather, it is at the expense of oneself. It is the pursuit of self-worth in the wrong place. Ultimately, self-validation does not come from sex, but it comes from God.

The quest for self-validation through sex, whether heterosexual or homosexual, leads to the death of the self. E. Lynn Harris has put us on the right track, however. The true self-validation is holistic, involving mind, body, spirit, and relationships. Connections with family and community are essential, and as Franklin points out, self-validation is a village process.

The clinical model has taught me not to jump on the contemporary debate about human sexuality with blinders. We need to be careful about too-easy solutions to one of our most complicated problems today. Our consumer-oriented culture can send us down a blind alley because the marketplace needs people to continue to seek self-validation through sex in order to function. Moreover, we need to learn to be patient in the debate over human sexuality, as Franklin advises, since heterosexuals, gays, and lesbians need one another's presence within the village and the church if we all are going to get on the right track in our quest for self-validation, which is ultimately found in relationship to God.

CHAPTER SEVEN

PERSONAL RESOURCES FOR DEVELOPING A NARRATIVE APPROACH

The narrative approach to pastoral care in the black church has been defined as drawing upon personal experience and the Bible for stories that might facilitate caring for those in need. Critically important to this process are several important skills. A major skill is the pastor's ability to have an "approachable," or perhaps "integrating," and conflict-free source for storytelling. This chapter explores the personal resources in a pastor's life that can offer a conflict- and anxiety-free source of narrative.

Since the appearance of *African American Pastoral Care* in 1991 there has been a subtle shift in the way I have looked at the use of the personal resources of the pastoral caregiver. The wounded healer was the center of my understanding of pastoral care, where the source of care came as a result of the caregiver being formed and shaped by his or her experiences with God healing one's wounds. Here again the emphasis on the wounded healer assumed that the village was intact and that the wounded healer was supported by the community as well as God in healing the wounds of others. As a result of the loss of the village as the contemporary reality, my thinking has shifted. Rather than placing more emphasis on the personal experience of the pastoral caregiver as the source of storytelling, I made a paradigm shift in my thinking to the role of the Bible as caregiver or as pastor.

The Bible as pastor or caregiver is a postmodern orientation growing out of a premodern understanding of the role of the faith community in healing. "One of the characteristics of the postmodern period is that we can reconsider premodern approaches to the use of traditional church resources for the growth and development of persons. Modernity, which is the result of the impact of the scientific revolution on the church and theology, made it difficult to appropriate pre-Enlightenment approaches to practical theology. More precisely, pre-Enlightenment sapient theology focused on the reality that being known by God positively impacted the growth and development and well-being of the knower," according to Ellen Charry.[1] The critical point is that it was the faith community that formed the pastoral caregiver, and the pre-Enlightenment community used doctrine and Scripture as communal resources for care. The key, then, is that the pastoral caregiver as storyteller needs to be viewed more as a representative of a community or as someone who stands within a faith community. When the pastoral caregiver draws on Scripture, the caregiver does so because the community or village is instrumental in the formation of the minister as biblical storyteller.

Our contemporary ethos with its emphasis on personal experience of the caregiver consistently points to the faith community and Scripture as sources of our storytelling. Those sources serve as important correctives to the imbalance brought about by an individualistic orientation.

Another important phenomenon emerged recently due to the Katrina and Rita hurricanes that caused so much devastation in New Orleans and on the Gulf Coast. While participating in helping clergy and their families tell stories as a way to heal the catastrophic losses in their lives, I realized that storytelling is not conflict-free, nor do people have to wait until they have healed their own wounds in order to begin healing one another. The caregivers' own healing and the sharing of their own pain as they live in the community after catastrophe can also contribute to the care of others. Being transparent about what they are experiencing as they journey through the significant losses can serve as an example of how to grieve and lament during loss. The use of the Bible as well as other stories that are not conflict-free will be addressed later in this chapter.

CONFLICT-FREE STORYTELLING

Although Katrina helped me see the significance of caregivers using the personal conflicts with which they are dealing as a source of care, conflict-free storytelling is still a major resource outside of catastrophic loss situations. Conflict-free storytelling refers to stories from the pastor's life and experience that have been so sufficiently worked through emotionally that the pastor can tell them without fear. In other words, the pastor can tell them without stirring up unresolved problems in his or her life that still need therapeutic attention. The anxiety-free storyteller is often a wounded healer whose own wounds have been sufficiently addressed, so that the stories emerging from the healing of personal wounds can be used as narrative. The storyteller should be one whose wounds have been healed to the extent that his or her story can be a source of another's healing.

A conflict-free storyteller also is aware of the major areas of ongoing personal conflict. There are areas in a pastor's close relationships and interactions with people that can continue to present problems. The pastor not only must be aware of these areas, but also must be able to keep these ongoing problems from interfering with the helpful ways he or she relates to the needs of others. A conflict-free storyteller is aware of ongoing problems in life and has found ways to prevent them from intruding into caring for others.

The major question is whether there are indigenous patterns within the black church where pastors can work together naturally to develop their abilities so as to be at ease with themselves as storytellers. There are natural settings where ministers gather to tell stories. The major concern in developing anxiety-free and conflict-free stories is finding a place where the pastor can tell personal stories. Following are examples of some ways pastors can involve themselves in telling personal stories in order to become conflict-free storytellers.

Since we assume that storytelling is the basic method of learning within the black culture, the implication is that black pastors must be able to share and reflect on the stories they tell, for the purpose of visualizing their healing value for themselves and others. They must have a setting in which they can tell stories to one another and, through this sharing, resolve personal anxiety as well as become conflict-free in their own minds. Such a setting needs to involve a trained specialist whom the pastors can draw on as a resource for personal healing as well as for counseling skills.

BIRTH MYTHOLOGY

One potential area of anxiety and conflict for pastors may be in the area of birth mythology. Birth mythology refers to the stories pastors hear about their own birth. For some pastors, these stories are an important source of nurture and growth; for other pastors, they are a present source of anxiety. But whether they are positive sources of identity and nurture or sources of anxiety, there needs to be a setting where these stories can be retold so that they no longer are threatening.

A brief review of the nature of birth mythology is helpful in explaining how these stories can be either nurturing or threatening. Birth mythology is composed of the stories one hears from parents and relatives concerning the circumstances surrounding one's birth. These circumstances include specific periods in the birth process, such as conception, time in the womb, the actual birth, the first months of life, and the religious dedication or infant baptism. Critical questions can help trigger the remembrance of the birth mythology in an adult: (1) What were the circumstances surrounding your conception? (2) Were you planned or unplanned? (3) What dreams and expectations did your parents have for you before you were born? (4) What was the first thing your mother said when she first saw you?

(5) What did your father say when he first saw you? (6) What was life like the first year you were born? (7) When, where, and why were you dedicated or baptized as an infant?

Of course, these questions can be answered by parents and other family members. What they say forms the basis of the birth mythology. That is to say, what we hear about our birth and the circumstances surrounding it is the foundation from which birth mythology springs. These stories are the roots of personal identity, as well as the primary sources of a child's God image.[2]

One illustration of a birth-mythology narrative is this story, told by one pastor to another:

> One of the earliest stories told about my life as a baby concerns how God used my mother and heard the prayers of the righteous to save me from a life-threatening condition.
>
> My mother became concerned about my "turning blue" and cries of pain when I was placed on my back. She also observed a growth on my head. Upon examining me, the doctor dismissed her concerns, saying she probably had dropped me on my head and that I really wasn't blue. I was pronounced normal and sent home.
>
> Mom persisted and brought me back repeatedly, traveling with her new son (her third child) on the bus in the cold Chicago winter, while her grandmother took care of my older sister and brother. On one such occasion, after one doctor, an intern, had told her that she had nothing to worry about, an experienced nurse stood behind the doctor and listened to his erroneous diagnosis.
>
> She said, "Lady, I'm not supposed to contradict the doctor, but he's just an intern and doesn't know what he is talking about. If you will bring your son back here tomorrow morning, I will make sure that he sees a specialist." The next morning, that specialist determined that there was a growth, and it was a sign of a dangerous blood clot that was moving toward my brain. When I was put on my back, more blood flowed to my head and caused me severe

pain. My "turning blue" was a result of this condition. I'm told that he gave me shots that very day to attempt to calcify the clot. The saints prayed that I would be healed and that I would not suffer brain damage. I look back on this story of my healing and on other occasions in which I could have lost my life, and I believe that God has given me the gift of life for a special purpose.

This pastor visualized from the stories told him that he was created for some special purpose. Through these stories, he was able to sense that he was a child of destiny and that his destiny was tied to God in some way. This gave him a sense of "somebodiness" as well as laid the foundation for his acceptance of a call to ministry. Moreover, he learned very early that there was a God who responded to people's prayers.

This pastor also envisaged a connection between the early stories he heard from his mother and the way they influenced his general outlook on life and his ministry. He saw suffering as part of life, but he sensed God's presence in the midst of life's difficulties.

He said, "By and large, people are still subject to problems of human existence. God is behind the dynamic force that both sustains and liberates people in the midst of suffering. Though healing and wholeness are possible with God, ultimate healing by God is found beyond time."

This birth mythology was a conflict-free and anxiety-free story that affected the pastor's outlook on life. It influenced everything he did from birth to the present. He saw it as a positive influence and as a positive source for his ministry, and because it was conflict- and anxiety-free, he was able to draw on it when necessary in caring for others.

Birth mythology is not always positive, however. There are situations when birth mythology is negative, and this negativity has a pejorative influence on the person's outlook on life. For example, one woman had a call to ministry, but because of the circumstances surrounding her birth, she had difficulty seeing herself as a minister. She had a feeling very early in her life that she was not a wanted child. When she began to wonder about the circumstances that surrounded her life, she found that her parents were in the midst of some serious marital problems when she was conceived. She felt that this had had a deleterious impact on her existence, and she saw life through pessimistic lenses and felt worthless. She managed to get herself into awkward situations where people would take advantage of her kindness, and consequently, she felt inadequate and hesitated to give a full commitment to ministry.

Fortunately, she told this story in a group of pastors who responded with concern and support. The sharing situation gave the pastors a chance to affirm her gifts and to support her—to attend her birth mythology. So that her birth mythology could become an anxiety- and conflict-free source of storytelling, they encouraged her to use the group, as well as other supportive caring and counseling resources, to help her become a wounded healer.

All pastors are wounded healers. Some have conflict- and anxiety-free birth mythologies; many do not. Yet, sharing birth mythologies in supportive environments can provide a first step in becoming a wounded healer, with a conflict- and anxiety-free mind. Having integrated one's own personal birth mythology into one's life, whether good or bad, one can then share that story with those in need.

CHILDHOOD STORIES, ROLES, AND RELATIONSHIPS

Another source of stories are those that pastors identified with as children. In these stories one can find sources for resolving conflict- and anxiety-laden problems that a child faces. Returning to these stories can be an excellent source of conflict-free narratives.

One pastor, as a child, identified with Moses in the Exodus story, and this story provided an early vision of what life should be like for African American people. He said, "Moses was a favorite because I learned to identify my own fight for justice through the Exodus story, and I was taught not to accept injustice. I saw very early the plight of black people through the eyes of the story of Moses and God's people."

Another pastor identified with other characters of the Bible who helped him gain important perspectives for developing a purpose in life:

I also liked David, because of the way he grew from being a little shepherd boy in the fields to prominence. As a young boy, I always found the whole story of David very fascinating. I learned that God could use very young people for God's purposes. I looked forward to the day when I could know what God wanted me to do with my life because of what I saw God doing through David.

This same pastor also said that he liked the stories of Paul:

Paul's conversation showed me that God would nurture and care for you as you moved into being a Christian. It showed that becoming a Christian was a growth process. I always had a sense of hope because of Paul. Through him, I knew I could continue to grow and be Christian, even though it seemed all those around me felt that becoming Christian happened all at once. Paul did have a sudden conversion, but he also lived his life in such a way that you could see how he also grew after the conversion.

Other pastors have identified with stories that helped them grow as children and youths, in spite of the obstacles. One pastor pointed out the importance of three Hebrew boys in his growth process:

When I was very young, I liked stories that were a challenge to me. I liked Shadrach, Meshach, and Abednego. I also liked to hear about Jesus teaching in the temple when he was only twelve years old. Shadrach and his friends, as youths, risked death for what they believed. And Jesus at the temple showed that at a young age individuals could do some awesome stuff.

As a child, I too was inspired by Bible stories, and by stories of my father's days at Bethune-Cookman College—when it was a two-year college and

Bethune had just merged with Cookman. My father often mentioned the faith of Mary McLeod Bethune. He proudly told how she built a black college on faith in God and how she knew that God would come through when money and resources for the institution were scarce. He also talked about her favorite story in the Bible, that of Esther, and how she saw herself and her mission through the story of Esther. From the stories my father told of Mary McLeod Bethune, I learned the importance of faith in life, particularly when working for God on behalf of your race.

African American women pastors also have found Bible stories important in shaping their identities. A female pastor in a Pentecostal denomination could not recall one favorite Bible story, but she indicated that thinking of herself as a person in ministry began when she encountered God in a vision early in her life. After feeling God's spirit move in her, she said that Esther became very important to her. Her orientation was toward God's movement in her life, and she sought to understand and interpret God's movement and presence through the use of Bible stories.

Another ordained pastor identified with the message of particular books of the Bible, rather than with particular characters. This pastor liked Exodus very early in her life because of its liberation themes. She saw God as the major actor in Exodus, leading God's people to freedom. She also liked the Gospel of Luke and the Letter to the Galatians. In Luke, she saw God respecting every person, whether male or female, slave or free. God and Jesus Christ were concerned with the least of these in society.

Many pastors I have interviewed identified, in their childhood, with stories and characters who helped them envision possibilities for their growth and development as persons. Some found that the perspective of the early stories carried them through their ministries. Those early stories became part of their lives and were a ready resource for stories that were anxiety- and conflict-free. The stories had positive plots, meaning that they had a positive direction, which facilitated personal growth. And because those plots led the pastors toward even further growth and development, they were also sources of anxiety- and conflict-free narratives.

At times, stories that pastors identify with are not helpful. I think of one pastor who identified with the Greek mythological character Sisyphus.[3] In Hades, Sisyphus was sentenced forever to roll a stone up a hill. Each time the stone almost reached the top of the hill, it became too heavy for him and it rolled back down, and Sisyphus would have to begin all over again.

For the pastor who identified with the tragic figure of Sisyphus to become a wounded healer, there was a need to find the kind of experiences that would help him edit this story that was shaping his life, a story that was not anxiety- or conflict-free. Some experiences had contributed to this view of life as a series of tragic, repeated endings and painful restarts, and this tragic scenario needed to be told in a caring storytelling environment, where it could be edited by feedback from supportive others. In its Greek mythological form, the story was inadequate for use in ministry; in order to use it as a positive resource in its edited form, the pastor needed to undergo some caring intervention.

Early role-playing, when a child takes on certain roles and functions within the home, can become a rich resource for anxiety- and conflict-free stories. One example is a woman who was an active participant in the life of her father's church. She had a speaking engagement in this church even as a little girl; as a preteen she often gave a speech or read a poem, and members of the congregation would respond with such comments as, "You really preached today!" This pastor had long talks with her father about the reaction of the congregation, and he was very supportive of her role in the life of the church. As a result of the support she received, she indicated that, at an early age, she knew that her life was not her own but that it belonged to God: "I can't remember not knowing God. But during my teenage years I started. I wrested with the thought of what I would do with my life, of what God wanted me to do. All through college I wrested with the idea of ministry. Consciously, I was not ready, but subconsciously, I was preparing for it."

This woman played significant roles within the life of the church. The support of others, and especially that of her father, contributed to building a faith structure that later matured when she decided to go into ministry.

Sometimes the roles played in childhood are not as positive as the one just cited. Negative roles, particularly those in which a child must assume adult responsibility prematurely, can become sources of anxiety and conflict. In such cases, it is the task of the wounded healers to gain sufficient separation from the negative roles so that they can freely choose an action response different from that prompted by the negative role. And a caring and loving environment of support is required in order to gain the ability to choose. When persons find themselves free from the negative roles, then as wounded healers, they can draw on those personal stories when caring for others.

Other significant sources of anxiety- and conflict-free stories are the relationships pastors had with those who were close to them early in their lives. An anxiety- and conflict-free relationship is one in which genuine care is offered by those concerned. One example is a female pastor who admired her minister father not only because he supported her in her desire to be a minister but also because he was a model father who built a positive relationship with her. He made himself available and was there when she needed him.

Positive relationships with mentors led some pastors to identify with the lives of their mentors and the stories they lived and told. Many pastors found a sense of self-esteem and worth in such relationships. This exchange and sharing of stories became a conflict-free reservoir for them. Not only did some pastors form positive relationships with their mentors, but many learned to tell stories with which their mentors identified. This meant that the pastors told stories they learned from their mentors, which ultimately helped them learn the narrative approach to life and ministry. But even when relationships with significant others were not good, many pastors found positive relationships with others within the church that more than made up for the tension that existed with some. Pastors have listed Christian teachers, coaches, and laypeople as persons who had positive influences on them.

THE PASTOR'S RESOURCES

The narrative context of the pastor's formative years, the birth mythology that surrounds the pastor's birth, the stories with which the pastor identifies early in life, the roles the pastor plays in life, and the quality of re-lationships with significant others all contribute to the development of a reservoir of healing, facilitative, conflict- and anxiety-free stories. But even when these areas are not conflict-free, they can be changed as the result of care and support from significant others, and such support enables the pastor to transform these areas into a reservoir for healing and caring. Through the transformation of the pastor's life, roles, stories, and relationships, he or she becomes a wounded healer with a reservoir of important stories.

Just as doctors should first "heal themselves," so pastors must support and help one another in a healing process, creating personal narratives that can be used to enlighten other narratives told by someone in need. The role of professional specialists and trainers in pastoral care and coun-seling is a must in helping the lives of pastors become conflict- and anxiety-free sources of stories.

TELLING STORIES DURING CATASTROPHIC CONFLICT

Pastors and their families are not immune from the losses and devas-tating impact of disastrous and catastrophic events.[4] Many congregations look to their pastoral leaders for answers to theological questions and con-cerns that these events are raising about the nature of God. Church mem-bers need a word from pastors on behalf of God. During catastrophic events, where there is devastating losses even for the pastor and his or her congregation, should pastors ignore their own reactions and reach out to others, neglecting themselves and their families? The answer is no. Pastors and their families must manage and come to grips with such events as any family would. The real problem is that we must manage our lives in the midst of tragedy while at the same time helping others face and manage their problems as well. The issue is that during catastrophic losses, con-gregations can benefit from the pastor and the pastor's family if the pastor and family are transparent about what they are experiencing and undergoing.

Facing catastrophic loss is not conflict-free. Conflict-free, earlier in this chapter, meant being free from the internal emotional and personal hang-ups so that the minister does not become a stumbling block to the effective care of another. Conflict-free in this sense is still important. What is crucial is that the pastor and his or her family must be emotionally mature enough to allow themselves to show how they are handling and coming to grips with monumental loss in ways that facilitate congregants to come to grips with their own losses with courage and "stand-fastness."

Because of the nature of the congregation as a family system, the congregation can benefit from the private way pastors and their families come to grips with catastrophic events. It is important for pastors, especially, to realize that there is value added to the lives of congregants when pastors genuinely show how hard it is to come to grips with devastating losses, how they don't hide their pain but face it with courage. Moreover, congregants also benefit from the pastors' and their families honesty that the situation is hard to deal with, but somehow they have found comfort in God's presence in their midst. This comfort, however, does not come through denying the pain. It is fully embracing pain, while discovering resilient practices in the midst of our pain. Resilient practices are defined as follows:

> The kind of resilience to which we are referring is a spiritual elasticity that is also borne of resilient faith in God's living and purpose-revealing presence. This kind of faith claims along the way, as Job did in the midst of mayhem, "I know that my Redeemer lives." And, this faith affirms that the message of divine purpose given by God to Judean exiles in Babylon recorded in the book of Jeremiah can be applied to the unique circumstances of clergy families today: "For I know the plans I have for you, says the Lord; plans for your welfare and not for harm, to give you a future with hope" (Jeremiah 29:11). Resilience is built by our claim that God not only has a plan and purpose for our unfolding story, but God also reveals the plotline on which we can count. God's plan and purpose are innermost aspects of the winds of promise. Resilience comes in God's

revealing God's plotline in ways that give direction in the throes of current circumstance and lead toward God's ends and purposes.[5]

Resilient practices grow out of the ability of clergy families to tell and retell stories. As they tell and retell stories in the midst of catastrophe, God's presence and plot become apparent. In fact, in *Winds of Promise* we outline a process of storytelling and retelling of stories that enables persons to discern God's unfolding plot in the midst of tragedy. We talk about the resilient practices of unmasking, inviting catharsis, relating empathically, unpacking the story, and discerning and deciding the way forward.[6] Unmasking is putting the challenges we are facing into storytelling form. That is, we give voice to what we are encountering in ways that recount one event and one scene at a time so that the events take on form and shape as the story unfolds. As the story unfolds, there are feelings that emerge, and resilience is born out of allowing and acknowledging those feelings. The practice of empathy is for each family member to attend to the feelings that are being expressed. It begins with the adults in the family facilitating the attending process by communicating that it is OK to express feelings. As the story unfolds, scene after scene, and the feelings get expressed, the desire to bring meaning to what is taking place naturally emerges in the storytelling process. Bringing meaning to the story involves examination of the beliefs and convictions that we have about what is taking place, the role of God in the process, and how God is leading us through the process. Finally, we begin to visualize how God is guiding us through the process and leading us forward. Thus, moving forward, then, is deciding to embrace what God is doing to help us move through what we are undergoing.

Congregants know almost intuitively how clergy and their families are doing when facing difficulties. Congregants can benefit from seeing pastors and their families embrace the various stages of the process. It comes through what pastors and their families share. Over time, the lives of the pastor and his or her family and the lives of the congregation converge and become one process of storytelling as they engage the different re-silient practices.

Perhaps the most helpful resilient practice is the practice of lamenting. Clergy families and congregants need to learn how to lament. Lament is a biblically and theologically sanctioned process of complaining directly to God about our circumstances. It is rooted in the psalms of lament as well as in Lamentations. Lament is not blasphemy. So far as I can tell, blas-phemy is denying that God cares about our predicament and, therefore, cursing God for not caring or doing anything about our circumstance and not expecting or wanting God to respond.[7] Lament, however, is com-plaining to God expecting God to hear us and respond. In fact, lament is an invitation for God to come into our lives and show us the way. There-fore, lament is an act of faith. It is a process through which we are able to discern the plot of God unfolding in our lives.

The story of Job is one of the best examples of lament. In fact, Job teaches us about the parameters of lament and how to approach God ex-pecting God to respond (Job 23:3-4). He said in faith that if he could lo-cate God he would lay out his case like a lawyer and God would plead his case. It is in our complaint that God shows up. It is in our plight that God offers us the gift of conversation. If we learn to privilege God conversa-tion or make what we hear from God in our lament primary, our circum-stances take on significant meaning.

CONCLUSION

In this chapter we updated the meaning of how the pastor is a major resource for doing pastoral care through telling and retelling of stories. The pastor and in some cases the pastor's family are conflict-free storytelling resources for care. Yet, this new edition focuses on the Bible as the primary pastor, showing us how it draws us into the unfolding plot of God to bring meaning in our lives. In fact, the Bible teaches us how to lament and in doing so links us with God's effort to bring meaning, hope, and guidance into our lives. In fact, it is in the midst of catastrophic circumstances that we can see God at God's best. That is, God offers us God's presence through conversation, and through conversation we experience the winds of promise as well as a way forward. Thus, this chapter enhanced the story-telling resources for pastoral care.

CHAPTER EIGHT

INDIGENOUS PASTORAL CARE

FACING THE TWENTY-FIRST CENTURY

Because African American oral culture has always used sharing stories in caring situations, this will remain a dominant approach in the African American church. However, the storytelling approaches that are emerging in counseling psychology might prove helpful to this indigenous approach in the future.

The spontaneous use of stories triggered in counseling relies on the right-brain processes of the caregiver's thinking. That is to say, the storytelling approach presented in this book relies heavily on the intuitive and imaginative capacities of the pastor or layperson, which are cultivated in oral cultures. Oral cultures emphasize emotion, celebration, poetic expression, relationships, storytelling, and story-listening.[1]

The focus of the model presented here is on stories that come spontaneously to the mind of the pastor or layperson, at the actual point of encounter with people or parishioners in need. The emphasis has been on telling stories that emerge as a result of what people are saying. That is, the pastors or laypeople tell stories—from their own lives, from their ministries, and from the Bible—that emerge because of something being experienced by those in need. The stories being told, therefore, are spontaneous events that emerge out of a reservoir of stories that is triggered in the encounter with the person in need. This triggering is an unconscious process, in which the person in need has an impact upon the caregiver, and the stories that emerge from the caregiver are shared with the person in need in facilitative ways that enable the person to grow.

An indigenous storytelling approach to pastoral care is learned by participating and living in an oral community, where hearing and speaking are very central. However, it cannot be taken for granted that this approach will remain viable and alive without some intentional effort. The more the dominant culture becomes visual—a seeing, reading, and writing culture—the greater the likelihood that oral indigenous approaches will lose some of their influence.

This chapter is an attempt to review some of the currrent literature on storytelling in counseling and its implication for an indigenous approach to pastoral care in the black church in the twenty-first century.

These words conclude the chapter introduction in the 1991 edition. Today, this introduction is still appropriate, but it needs to be updated. The update is that the village has collapsed all over the world, and there are several models that need to be added. In fact, there are three models. For example, there is the model called the "definitional ceremony." Australian family therapist Michael White introduced this concept, drawn from his work with Aboriginal people as he helped them cope with bereavement after their traditional culture had been destroyed by the impact of industrial and technological advances. The second model actually includes several different models of re-villaging, and the third model is "Bible as pastor." Each one of these models has emerged recently but has a narrative base.

OTHER RELATED MODELS

The new therapeutic approaches to storytelling rely on assessment of the caring needs of persons from the perspectives of developmental psychology and personality theory. These approaches use psychological theories of counseling, in conjunction with theories of human growth, to suggest how to use storytelling. In addition, some storytelling theories outline complex structures that match the story to the phase of counseling and the need of the person.

One model focuses on sharing stories at particular points in the counseling process.[2] These specific points include goal-setting, focusing on specific developmental and behavioral problems, and addressing family problems. The idea behind the use of stories is to evoke ideas, feelings, attitudes, and attention to relationships that facilitate the counseling. This approach also outlines specific steps in story creation that reflect the specific problem being addressed.

Another approach assumes that people rework unresolved conflict by acting out specific themes in stories.[3] The goal in this approach is to affect the themes that people are acting out in resolving problems by helping the counselees identify the actual story themes that are related to conflict. Once these themes are identified, counselors design strategies for influencing the stories that have given rise to the conflicts. The goal of influencing these stories is to help the counselees develop more growth-facilitating themes, myths, and self-definitions. Storytelling is a major means of influencing the existing stories and themes in the counselee's life.

Still another storytelling model designs stories based on treatment goals.[4] In this goal-oriented approach, once the goals for counseling are set, counselors explore their experience for stories similar to those of the counselees. When these are identified in the counselor's life, stories are constructed to help achieve the goals that have been set. This approach relies on protocols, or carefully structured stories to meet the goals of the counseling. These protocols focus on the development of stories around characters, relationships, movements, feelings, or behaviors.

In addition to these varied approaches in therapy, there are also various approaches to Bible storytelling. One such approach focuses on structuring stories based on the natural rhythm of the story.[5] This helps the pastor and layperson construct biblical stories based on the internal structure of the story itself.

The model that this new edition introduces is the Bible as pastor approach. This approach focuses on the ability of the Bible to draw people into itself and disclose a new plot for those who encounter it in ways that give meaning. The role of the pastoral caregiver, whether as an individual or part of a larger group, is to make sure there is a comfortable atmosphere for encountering biblical stories. I define the Bible as pastor approach in the following way:

> The Bible functions as pastor when it discloses meaning, purpose, worth, value, dignity, identity and wisdom to people, who bring to the encounter between themselves, biblical texts and God, personal, communal, and sociopolitical questions and concerns about the meaning of life in a world of injustice, oppression, and evil. The Bible as pastor is also about people being shaped and formed by the encounter between God and biblical texts so that they become virtuous people participating faithfully in the coming of God's rule and reign on earth. It is from the encounter of the listener/reader of biblical texts with God and the texts while participating within faith communities that true transformation of persons and community take place. In short, the Bible as pastor is all about forming and shaping persons to engage in the transformation of all life related to the coming of God's rule and reign on earth.[6]

A GOAL-ORIENTED MODEL

With the exception of the Bible as pastor approach, the approaches described above have implications for an indigenous storytelling approach to pastoral care as we face the twenty-first century. They suggest that one specific direction lies in preplanning stories, and they offer specifics for ways this can be done. There is some value to preplanning stories, even if one does not have an opportunity to use them, since one can build one's repertoire of stories to be drawn on when needed. Second, preplanning can increase the storytelling facility of the caregiver, so that when stories are told, they can be more useful to those in need of care.

The approach I want to emphasize is the goal-oriented approach—addressing a particular counseling goal through the use of story. In this approach, counselors first identify the goal and then begin to explore their own experience to discover a story similar to that of the counselee. When such a story is identified, the process of building a story for counseling begins.

Although the goal-oriented model is a preplanning model, it focuses on the personal experiences and life of the counselor, so this approach actually is similar to the indigenous approach to storytelling described in this book. The goal-oriented model can serve as a method for constructing stories that can be used in counseling as well as in other settings. While the indigenous storytelling approach grows naturally out of an oral culture, one can rehearse and build stories in many settings within an oral culture, and the goal-oriented model lends itself to those natural occasions.

The central building block for the goal-oriented model is the protocol—a standard procedure, a map, a set of guidelines—that can be followed in building a story to facilitate the accomplishment of a particular goal. When building a story with the protocol method, the counselor must have in mind the goal that the story needs to address. The goal could involve attitudes that need challenging, feelings that need to be expressed, some behavior that needs to be enhanced or modified, a perspective that needs to be influenced, or some decision that needs to be made.[7] Once the goal has been identified, the counselors can plumb their own experiences for stories that are possibilities for story-building to meet the goal.

The protocol for building stories usually has several steps. The first phase is the exploration of the presenting problem, the initial concern that has led the person to counseling at this particular time.

Once the problem is presented within its social and interpersonal context, general information is gathered. This second phase includes helping the counselee gain a larger perspective of the presenting problem by exploring it from various psychological assessment models. This phase usually ends when counseling goals are established, based on assessment of the needs of the counselee. These goals, agreed upon between the counselor and the counselee, include the problem the counselee desires to address in the counseling—the desired changes in feelings, attitude, perspective, behavior, and identity that the person wants to accomplish.

The third phase begins when the goals are set and the counseling process moves toward accomplishing the established goals.[8] In this phase, pastoral counselors turn their attention to the unfolding story of the counselee. If the need for storytelling arises, counselors need to have in mind the steps for building a story based on the protocol:

Step 1: Explore their own lives and situations for stories that might be similar to the desired goals that have been established.

Step 2: Choose a main character, or several main characters, who have problems and goals similar to those of the counselee.

Step 3: Choose a character or situation and build a story, developing in detail the character or situation that introduces the desired changes required by the counseling goal. The key is to stimulate the imagination of the listener.

Step 4: Explore in detail the consequences for the main characters in achieving or not achieving the desired goals. This step must show that there are consequences in accomplishing or not accomplishing the desired goals.

The protocol helps pastoral counselors develop stories based on the established counseling goals. It also helps the storyteller develop specific characters, contexts, and plots that can trigger the imagination of the counselee. It must be emphasized that learning to tell stories in this way requires training and supervision in basic counseling skills, including building rapport, empathy, assessment of psychological and interpersonal dynamics, and the phases of counseling. Such training should be in the form of courses, as well as in actual practice and in reflection on that practice with experienced trainers. Training will enhance pastors' ability to deliver quality care to parishioners, as well as strengthen the pastors' own personal and emotional growth.

Following is one example of the use of a protocol to develop a story to achieve a certain counseling goal. This example contains the three protocol steps: (1) It addresses a perspective that must be changed, challenged, or explored in the main character's life; (2) it introduces an opposite perspective through a different character; and (3) it relates the consequences of each character's perspectives.[9]

I once counseled a man who had a very negative outlook on life. He felt his life was doomed, that there was no hope for him. Laboring under the weight of difficult memories, he saw very little chance to undo their impact. As he talked, the Bible story of Joseph's betrayal by his brothers came to me. I decided to take some time to read that story again and plan a protocol for telling the story to the counselee at a later date, with his need in mind. The goal was to address his gloom-and-doom perspective and help him envision possibilities in the midst of difficulty. When we met for our next appointment, I related this story:

> Two people were reading the story of Joseph in the book of Genesis. The story goes that Joseph was his father's favorite son, and the father loved him so much that he made him a special coat. Joseph's brothers saw how their father treated him and were very jealous. They decided that all their lives would be different if Joseph were not around, so they seized an opportunity and put him into a deep well where he would never be found.
>
> However, when some slave traders came by, the brothers decided to rescue him from the well and sell him into slavery. They took Joseph's coat and dipped it in the blood of an animal they had killed. Then they took the bloodied coat to their father and told him that Joseph had been torn apart by an animal. The father was grief-stricken, but Joseph was no longer around to anger his brothers by receiving their father's favored treatment.

The first person who read this account became depressed and put the book down. He refused to read any further, pointing out that life was nothing but a bunch of disappointments and that people, particularly family members, will betray you and keep on abusing you. He stopped reading, feeling that the plot had ended and Joseph was doomed to an endless life of slavery.

The second reader did not stop reading when Joseph was sold into slavery. She had a feeling that the story was unfolding chapter by chapter, and it would be too bad to stop reading before the entire story was finished. She made up her mind to follow the story episode by episode until she came to the dramatic end.

The next episode picked up after Joseph had been in slavery for some time. He was found to be a good and faithful manager. He came to the attention of the ruler, who put Joseph in charge of all his household and domestic affairs.

The second reader noticed that Joseph had made the best of an unfortunate situation. Although he had been abused by his brothers and treated inhumanly, he was able to become indispensable to the new ruler.

The story continued with the introduction of the ruler's wife, who had noticed that Joseph was handsome and very strong. She had a romantic interest in him and made several unsuccessful attempts to get him to go to bed with her. Joseph was a very responsible person who had been entrusted with the entire household. He refused her advances, telling her that such action would undermine the trust that her husband had placed in him. But she would not take no for an answer. She clutched at him. With a quick maneuver he was free from her grasp, but she had grabbed his coat. Then, with coat in hand, she called her attendants and reported that Joseph had attacked her.

The second reader was very disappointed with the way this episode had turned out. An unfortunate event had caused the story to take a different turn. The plot thickened, and the positive became negative. The second reader wanted to stop reading. She had become discouraged, but she decided to read on, realizing that the story was not quite over.

In the next episode, the ruler cast Joseph into prison. Part of the difficulty between Joseph and his brothers in the beginning was caused by a dream he had interpreted to his brothers. In the dream, he was ruling over his brothers. Of course, his brothers resented this, and one consequence of his arrogance was that he was sold into slavery. The point of this brief interpretative interlude is that Joseph was a dreamer and an interpreter of dreams. And eventually it was this God-given talent that became the central element in Joseph's prison life.

Confined with Joseph while he was in prison were two other people—a baker and a cupbearer for the ruler. Joseph interpreted their dreams, and both those interpretations predicted events that later actually occurred. The baker met with an unfortunate political death. But the cupbearer was returned to his former job, and Joseph begged him to bring his continued imprisonment to the attention of the ruler. The cupbearer promised that he would remember Joseph to the ruler as soon as possible.

The second reader was encouraged by this possible twist of Joseph's story toward a positive end, and she read on with great anticipation.

The setting for the next episode changed from the prison to the ruler's court. Several years had elapsed, and the cupbearer, who had access to the ruler, had forgotten all about Joseph and the promise he had made. However, when the king had a puzzling dream, the cupbearer remembered Joseph and told the ruler of his ability to interpret dreams. The ruler already knew Joseph and had confidence in him because of his previous experience. Joseph was released from prison and interpreted the ruler's dream.

The second reader was overjoyed by this sudden change in Joseph's fate, but when she discovered there was more to the story, she wondered again what the future might hold. Suspense began to build as she continued to allow the story to unfold, not knowing where it might lead.

Joseph was put in charge of the ruler's department of agriculture. Since the interpretation of the dream involved a prediction of many years of plentiful crops, prior to many years of drought, the ruler knew of no one better to plan for the years of drought. Joseph set to work and managed the agricultural system, putting aside food during the years of plenty so that the nation could prepare for the years of drought.

When the years of drought came, the ruler and his people were well prepared because of Joseph's dream interpretation and his administrative and management skills. However, Joseph's father and brothers were not as fortunate. His brothers came for food, but they did not know that it was Joseph they were asking to give them food. Joseph's father was not with the brothers when they came, but Joseph found a way to keep one of his brothers with him while the others were sent home to bring back the father. When the father came back with the other brothers, Joseph told them who he was, and there was a glorious reunion.

The first reader's world remained the same, since that person stopped reading about Joseph after the first episode. But the second reader's life was profoundly changed by the story. By following the unfolding plot, the second reader came to realize that difficult circumstances do not always determine the outcome of events. The second reader learned to read life as an unfolding drama whose outcome one cannot predict until it actually happens. Tragic beginnings don't always have tragic endings.

This story was designed to address the goal—to influence the gloom-and-doom attitude of the counselee. The story was biblical and preplanned to address the attitude through a protocol using two different characters.

The Bible as pastor approach differs from the above use of the protocol to design stories. The protocol approach relies on the pastoral imagination of the pastoral counselor and his or her ability to design creative and innovative approaches. In the Bible as pastor, the approach relies on the disclosing power of Scripture itself in drawing the reader into the text, and Scripture and the reader become engaged. The role of the pastoral caregiver is less strategic and more related to being sure that he or she is not intrusive so as to interrupt the encounter between the text and the person. The Bible as pastor is more related to the work I did in *Using Scripture in Pastoral Counseling*, where the reader identifies with one of the characters and as a result takes on the plot of the story and is transformed.[10]

LIFE IN THE TWENTY-FIRST CENTURY

Storytelling is an art. Some of the clues for this art already exist in African American culture. However, as we continue to be changed by technology, we will need to integrate the natural community traditions with intentional methods in order to recover and keep alive traditions that will be influenced by technology. Storytelling within African American tradition is alive and well in black churches, yet traditional patterns of care through the use of storytelling are being challenged by such societal influences as the erosion of the extended family.

The major concern for the future is to maintain the indigenous, spontaneous form of caring through stories that exist in the African American tradition. However, we can learn to preserve and enhance this tradition through studying the emerging literature on storytelling. We need to take pride that the academic and professional world of counseling is rediscovering what was already a full-blown tradition in African American culture.

Now that we are clearly in the twenty-first century, it is clear that the indigenous storytelling tradition still exists, but the traditions of the village, which once buttressed this tradition, have collapsed. Thus, new models of storytelling need to exist that take into full consideration the fact that traditions once supporting the indigenous storytelling tradition are gone. One such strategic method has been developed by Michael White and is known as the definitional ceremony; other traditions are models provided from Zimbabwe where the village functions are being re-created in the village as well as several other methods my wife and I developed in the mid 1990s.

Michael White uses a practice called the Definitional Ceremony that is used when villages and their culture have been destroyed by Western industry and technology. Village functions are those functions that help people maintain emotional, spiritual, and interpersonal integrity when communal ties are being threatened. The definitional ceremony is a method of indigenous storytelling. The method strategically intervenes in the lives of persons whose traditions have collapsed, and the persons are facing crises and circumstances where they need to tell their stories. Michael has these persons tell their stories to a small group of people. He says:

> The definitional ceremonies that I am referring to here usually take place in structured forums, which provide a space for persons to engage in expressions of the stories of their lives—these might be stories about their personal projects, about work, about their identity and so on—and for the expression of the knowledge of life and skills of living that are associated with these stories. These expressions constitute a performance that is witnessed by an audience, one that is specially convened for this purpose. Following the performance, the outsider-witness group is invited to respond with a re-telling of the stories told and of the knowledge and skills expressed. At this time (the second stage), the persons who are at the center of the ceremony participate as an audience to these re-tellings. The re-tellings of the outsider—witness group—have the effect of rescuing the said from the saying of it (Geertz 1973), the told from the telling of it.[11]

After the telling and the retelling, both the first teller and the audience engage a process of reflection so that the storytellers learn new knowledge and skills that they can then incorporate into their lives and their networks. This enables people to re-experience their cultural heritage. They form key rituals, texts, myths, narratives, and drama that are constitutive and shaping of culture.[12]

A similar model re-creating the village functions is found in Zimbabwe. They are called sections. Sections are cross-generational gatherings that take place in the urban areas of Zimbabwe where the village life is re-created within local congregations and neighborhoods. These gatherings are designed to carry out the symbolic, ritualistic, maintenance, reparative, and meditative functions of the village.[13] The village functions are defined as follows:

> Ritualistic functions refer to those repetitive patterns of communal life that reinforce the village worldview and values and that assist persons' movement through life transitions. Maintenance functions refer to those support systems, practices, and values that help people maintain themselves holistically when encountering the problems of life. Reparative functions are those healing endeavors in which the community engages after someone has been hurt or broken. Mediating functions are those mechanisms that transmit the worldview and spiritual values from one generation to the next. Nurture and care embrace all of these functions. As such, nurture and care can be significant in helping recover the needed role of the village.[14]

NOTES

Preface to Revised Edition

1. Robert C. Dykstra, *Images of Pastoral Care: Classic Readings* (St. Louis: Chalice Press, 2005), 155-56.

2. Henry Mitchell and Nicholas Lewter, *Soul Theology* (New York: Harper & Row, 1986).

3. Homer U. Ashby Jr., *Our Home Is Over Jordan* (St. Louis: Chalice Press, 2003).

4. Cornel West, *Race Matters* (New York: Vintage Books, 1993), 22-24.

5. Dykstra, *Images of Pastoral Care*, 155-56.

6. Michel Foucault, *The Archaeology of Knowledge and the Discourse on Language* (New York: Pantheon Books, 1972), 51-52.

7. Dykstra, *Images of Pastoral Care*, 155-56.

8. The Bible as Pastor Movement emerged out of a joint project between the Bible Society and the School of Religious and Theological Studies, Cardiff University, Cardiff, Wales in 2000, concerned with the gulf between the work of biblical scholars and practical theologians. My own contribution to this discussion was made in September 2005 at a conference entitled the Bible as Pastor, and my contribution is entitled "An African American Perspective," in the periodical called *Contact Practical Theology and Pastoral Care: The Bible as Pastor* (Cardiff, Wales: Cardiff University Press, 2006), 18-25.

9. Rodney Hunter, "The Bible in Pastoral Practice: Themes and Challenges," *Contact: Practical Theology and Pastoral Care: The Bible as Pastor* (Cardiff, Wales: Cardiff University Press, 2006), 4-7.

I. A Narrative Approach to Pastoral Care

1. Henry Mitchell and Nicholas Lewter, *Soul Theology* (New York: Harper & Row, 1986), 11.

2. Ibid., 3.

3. James Hillman, *Healing Fiction* (Barrytown, N.Y.: Station Hill, 1983), 9-12.

4. Mitchell and Lewter, *Soul Theology*, 14.

5. See James Hopewell, *Congregations, Stories, and Structures* (Philadelphia: Fortress Press, 1987), 154.

6. These functions are defined in Edward P. Wimberly, *Pastoral Care in the Black Church* (Nashville: Abingdon Press, 1979), 18-23.

7. Michael White, *Narratives of Therapists' Lives* (Adelaide, South Australia: Dulwich Centre Publications, 1997), 93.

8. Edward P. Wimberly, Anne Streaty Wimberly, and Annie Grace Chingonzo, "Pastoral Counselling, Spirituality and the Recovery of the Village Functions: African and African-American Correlates in the Practice of Pastoral Care and Counselling," in *Spirituality and Culture in Pastoral Care and Counseling*, John Fosket and Emmanuel Lartey, eds (Cardiff, Wales: Cardiff Academic Press, 2004), 16-17.

9. Ibid., 16.

10. White, *Narrative of Therapists' Lives*, 93.

II. Pastoral Care and Worship

1. Freebasing, converting cocaine into a smokable form sometimes known as crack, is one of the purest forms of using cocaine and is very addictive. Smoking cocaine enables the drug to reach the brain in eight to ten seconds. The high is short-lived, lasting only two to five minutes. The crash is intense and happens abruptly. Freebasing stimulates craving, and many addicts go on binges known as a "run," which can cost as much as $1,000 a day, leaving the addict in a total state of confusion. Psychiatric symptoms include paranoia, severe depression, and emotional volatility. Other risks include brain seizure, respiratory failure, and heart attack. See Arnold M. Washton, *Cocaine Addiction: Treatment, Recovery and Relapse Prevention* (New York: W. W. Norton & Co., 1989), 14-16.

III. Pastoral Care and Support Systems

1. This definition is contained in Erich Lindemann, "Symptomatology and Management of Acute Grief," *Crisis Intervention*, ed. Howard J. Parad (New York: Family Service Association, 1976), 7.

2. See Lindemann, "Symptomatology of Acute Grief," 7-21, for his reference to basic tasks for the bereaved.

3. Ibid.

4. Ibid.

5. John Bowlby, "Pathological Mourning and Childhood Mourning," *Journal of the American Psychoanalytic Association* 11 (July 1963): 501.

6. Murray C. Parkes, "Seeking and Finding a Lost Object: Evidence from Recent Studies of the Reaction to Bereavement," *Social Science and Medicine* 4 (1970): 187-201.

7. Bowlby, "Pathological Mourning," 505.

8. For readings in African pastoral care and counseling, see Abraham Adu Berinyuu, *Towards Theory and Practice of Pastoral Counseling in Africa* (Frankfurt: Peter Lang, 1989), 82-98; *Pastoral Care to the Sick in Africa* (Frankfurt: Peter Lang, 1988); Masamba ma Mpolo, "African Pastoral Care Movement," and "African Traditional Religion, Personal Care In," *Dictionary of Pastoral Care and Counseling* (Nashville: Abingdon Press, 1990), 11-12, 12-13.

9. Anne E. Streaty Wimberly and Edward Powell Wimberly, *The Winds of Promise: Building and Maintaining Strong Clergy Families* (Nashville: Discipleship Resources, 2007) 35-50.

10. "Special Report from the Gulf Coast," *ColorsNW Magazine* (Nov 2005) at http://www.colorsnw.com/cover_story.html, 11/3/2005.

11. Ibid.

IV. Pastoral Care and Life Crises

1. Edward P. Wimberly, *A Conceptual Model for Pastoral Care* (Ann Arbor: University of Michigan Microfilms, 1976), 69-74.

2. Edward P. Wimberly, "The Family Context of Development: African American Families," in *Human Development and Faith: Life-Cycle Stages of Body, Mind, and Soul*, Felicity B. Kelcourse, ed. (St. Louis: Chalice Press, 2004), 111-25.

3. Ibid.

4. Ibid.

5. Ibid., 113.

6. Ibid., 112.

7. Erik Eckholm, "Plight Deepens for Black Men, Studies Warn," nytimes.com. March 20, 2006.

8. Edward P. Wimberly, *Relational Refugees: Alienation and Reincorporation in African American Churches and Communities* (Nashville: Abingdon Press, 2000).

9. Erik Eckholm, "Plight Deepens for Black Men, Studies Warn," nytimes.com. March 20, 2006.

10. Ronald B. Mincy, *Black Males Left Behind* (Washington D.C.: Urban Institute Press, 2006).

11. Peter Edelman et al., *Reconnecting Disadvantaged Young Men* (Washington, D. C.: Urban Institute Press, 2006).

12. Sylvia Ann Hewlett and Cornel West, *The War Against Parents: What We Can Do for America's Beleaguered Moms and Dads* (New York: Houghton Mifflin, 1998), 144-45.

13. White, Richelle B., *Daughters of Imani: A Christian Rites of Passage Program for African American Young Women* (Nashville: Abingdon Press, 2005), 98.

14. Marv Penner, *My Kids Are Hurting: A Survival Guide to Working with Students in Pain* (Grand Rapids: Zondervan, 2005), 134.

15. David M. Schnarch, *Constructing the Sexual Crucible: An Integration of Sexual and Marital Therapy* (New York: W. W. Norton, 1991), 187.

16. See Erik H. Erikson, *Childhood and Society* (New York: W. W. Norton, 1963), 65.

17. Pamela Cooper-White, "Human Development in Relational and Cultural Context," in *Human Development and Faith*, Felicity Kelcourse, ed. (St. Louis: Chalice Press, 2004), 98-99.

18. Wimberly, *Relational Refugees*, 93-106.

19. Ibid., 64-73.

V. Premarriage, Marriage, and Family Counseling

1. See Dennis A. Bagarozzi and Stephen A. Andersen, *Personal, Marital, and Family Myths* (New York: W. W. Norton, 1989).

2. Robert M. Franklin, *Crisis in the Village: Restoring Hope in African American Communities* (Minneapolis: Fortress Press, 2007), 46.

3. Ibid., 53.

4. Ibid., 54-59.

5. Ibid., 43.

6. Ibid.

7. Herbert G. Gutman, *The Black Family in Slavery and Freedom 1750–1925* (New York: Vintage Books, 1976), 558-59.

8. E. Hammon Oglesby, *Pressing Toward the Mark: Christian Ethics for the Black Church Today* (Eugene, Oreg.: Wipf and Stock, 2007).

9. Ibid., 21.

10. Charles Gerkin, *Crisis Experience in Modern Life: Theory and Theology for Pastoral Care* (Nashville: Abingdon Press, 1979).

VI. Pastoral Care and Human Sexuality

1. David M. Schnarch, *Constructing the Sexual Crucible: An Integration of Sexual and Marital Therapy* (New York: W. W. Norton and Company, 1991), 557.

2. Edward P. Wimberly, "Pastoral Care and Sexual Diversity in the Black Church," in *Pastoral Care and Counseling in Sexual Diversity* (New York: The Haworth Pastoral Press, 2001), 45.

3. Ibid., 46.

4. Ibid., 50.

5. Ibid., 46.

6. Robert M. Franklin, *Crisis in the Village: Restoring Hope in African American Communities* (Minneapolis: Fortress Press, 2007), 45.

7. Ibid., 40.

8. Wimberly, "Pastoral Care and Sexual Diversity," 47.

9. Ibid., 48.

10. Rudy Rasmus, *Touch: The Power of Touch in Transforming Lives* (Friendswood, Tex. and Houston, Tex.: Baxter Press and Spirit Rising, 2006), 17.

11. Schnarch, *Constructing the Sexual Crucible*, 93.

12. For a discussion on the meaning of shame today, see the following sources: Edward P. Wimberly, *Moving from Shame to Self-Worth: Preaching and Pastoral Care* (Nashville: Abingdon Press, 1999), 39-40, 51-52, 57-58, 61-62, 65-66, 75; Leon Wurmser, *The Mask of Shame* (Baltimore: Johns Hopkins University Press, 1981); John Patton, *Is Human Forgiveness Possible?* (Nashville: Abingdon Press, 1985); Gershen Kaufman, *The Psychology of Shame: Theory and Treatment of Shame Based Syndromes* (New York: Springer, 1989).

13. Wimberly, *Moving from Shame to Self-Worth*, 11.

14. Ibid., 120-22.

15. Ibid., 122.

16. Wimberly, "Pastoral Care and Sexual Diversity," 53.

17. *The Interpreter's Dictionary of the Bible* vol. 3 (Nashville: Abingdon Press, 1991), 43.

18. This case is found in Wimberly, "Pastoral Care and Sexual Diversity," 55-56.

19. E. Lynn Harris, *What Becomes of the Brokenhearted* (New York: Doubleday, 2003).

20. Ibid., 204.

21. Ibid., 235, 246.

22. Franklin, *Crisis in the Village*, 89-92.

23. Ibid., 91.

24. Edward P. Wimberly, "Race and Sex in the Debate over Homosexuality in the United Methodist Church," in *Staying the Course: Supporting the Church's Position on Homosexuality* (Nashville: Abingdon Press, 2003), 153-58.

25. http://en.wikipedia.org/wiki/United_Methodist_Church, May 6, 2007.

26. Franklin, *Crisis in the Village*, 45.

27. Wimberly, "Race and Sex in the Debate over Homosexuality in the United Methodist Church," 154-55.

28. Robert Jewett, *Romans: A Commentary* (Minneapolis: Fortress Press, 2007).

29. Ibid., 428.

30. Ibid., 436.

31. Ibid., 437.

VII. Personal Resources for Developing a Narrative Approach

1. The quotation came from a lecture that I gave entitled "The Bible as Pastor: An African American Perspective" at Cardiff University, Cardiff, Wales, September 5-7, 2005.

2. Dennis A. Bagarozzi and Stephen A. Anderson, *Personal, Marital, and Family Myths* (New York: W. W. Norton, 1989), 22-41.

3. For the details see Edward P. Wimberly, "Spiritual Formation in Theological Education and Psychological Assessment," *Clergy Assessment and Career Development*, ed. Richard A. Hunt, John E. Hinkle, and H. Newton Malony (Nashville: Abingdon Press, 1990), 30-31.

4. This section is built on the book written by my wife and me entitled *The Winds of Promise: Building and Maintaining Strong Clergy Family* (Nashville: Discipleship Resources, 2007).

5. Ibid., 29.

6. Ibid, 37-49.

7. Edward P. Wimberly, *Claiming God, Reclaiming Dignity: African American Pastoral Care* (Nashville: Abingdon Press, 2003), 113-14.

VIII. Indigenous Pastoral Care

1. For a description of the significance of oral cultures, see Clarence J. Rivers, "The Oral African Tradition Versus the Ocular Tradition," *This Far by Faith: American Black Culture and Its African Roots* (Washington, D.C.: The National Office of Black Catholics, 1977), 38-49.

2. See Philip Barker, *Using Metaphors in Psychotherapy* (New York: Brunner & Mazel, 1985).

3. See Dennis A. Bagarozzi and Stephen A. Anderson, *Personal, Marital, and Family Myths* (New York: W. W. Norton, 1989).

4. See Carol H. Lankton and Stephen R. Lankton, *Tales of Enchantment: Goal-oriented Metaphors for Adults and Children in Therapy* (New York: Brunner & Mazel, 1989).

5. Thomas E. Boomershine, *Story Journeying: An Invitation to the Gospel as Storytelling* (Nashville: Abingdon Press, 1988).

6. Edward P. Wimberly, "The Bible as Pastor: An African American Perspective," Cardiff University, Cardiff, Wales, September 5-7, 2007.

7. Lankton and Lankton, *Tales of Enchantment*, 7, 27-28.

8. For details on the three phases of the counseling process, see Gerard Egan, *The Skilled Helper* (Pacific Grove, Calif.: Brooks Kole, 1990), 28-53.

9. Ibid., 71.

10. See Edward P. Wimberly, *Using Scripture in Pastoral Counseling* (Nashville: Abingdon Press, 1994).

11. Michael White, *Narratives of Therapist's Lives* (Adelaide, South Australia: Dulwich Centre Publications, 1997), 94.

12. Ibid., 95.

13. Edward P. Wimberly, Anne Streaty Wimberly, and Annie Grace Chingonzo, "Pastoral Counselling, Spirituality and the Recovery of the Village Functions: African and African-American Correlates in the Practice of Pastoral Care and Counselling," in *Spirituality and Culture in Pastoral Care and Counselling* (Cardiff, Wales: Cardiff Academic Press, 2004), 15-30.

14. Ibid., 16.

BIBLIOGRAPHY

Ali, Carroll A. Watkins. *Survival and Liberation: Pastoral Theology in African American Context.* St. Louis: Chalice Press, 1999.

Ashby, Homer U. *Our Home Is Over Jordan: A Black Pastoral Theology.* St. Louis: Chalice Press, 2003.

Bagarozzi, Dennis A., and Stephen A. Anderson, *Personal, Marital, and Family Myths.* New York: W. W. Norton, 1989.

Barker, Philip. *Using Metaphors in Psychotherapy.* New York: Brunner & Mazel, 1985.

Berinyuu, Abraham. *Pastoral Care to the Sick in Africa: An Approach to Transcultural Pastoral Theology.* Frankfurt: Peter Lang, 1988.

Birchett, Colleen, ed. *How to Help Hurting People.* Chicago: Urban Ministries, Inc., 1990.

Boomershine, Thomas E. *Story Journeying: An Invitation to the Gospel as Storytelling.* Nashville: Abingdon Press, 1988.

Bowlby, John. "Pathological Mourning and Childhood Mourning." In *Journal of the American Psychoanalytic Association* 11 (July 1963): 501.

Butler, Lee H. *A Loving Home: Caring for African American Marriage and Families.* Cleveland: Pilgrim Press, 2000.

_____. *Toward Theory and Practice of Pastoral Counseling in Africa.* Frankfurt: Peter Lang, 1989.

Cooper-White, Pamela. "Human Development in Relational and Cultural Context." In *Human Development and Faith*, edited by Felicity Kelcourse, 98-99. St. Louis: Chalice Press, 2004.

Dykstra, Robert C. *Images of Pastoral Care: Classic Readings.* St. Louis: Chalice Press, 2005.

Eckholm, Erik. "Plight Deepens for Black Men, Studies Warn," nytimes.com. March 20, 2006.

Edelman, Peter et al. *Reconnecting Disadvantaged Young Men.* Washington, D.C.: Urban Institute Press, 2006.

Egan, Gerard. *The Skilled Helper.* Pacific Grove, Calif.: Brooks Kole, 1990.

Erikson, Erik H. *Childhood and Society.* New York: W. W. Norton, 1963.

Felton, Carroll M., Jr. *The Care of Souls in the Black Church*. New York: Martin Luther King Fellows Press, 1980.

Foucault, Michel. *The Archaeology of Knowledge and the Discourse of Language*. New York: Pantheon Books, 1972.

Franklin, Robert M. *Crisis in the Village: Restoring Hope in African American Communities* (Minneapolis: Fortress Press, 2007).

Gerkin, Charles. *Crisis Experience in Modern Life: Theory and Theology for Pastoral Care*. Nashville: Abingdon Press, 1979.

Harris, E. Lynn. *What Becomes of the Brokenhearted*. New York: Doubleday, 2003.

Hartsfield, Amy H. "Identity Formation/Change in African-American Women." In *The Journal of The Interdenominational Theological Center* (Spring 1998): 85-109.

Hewlett, Sylvia Ann, and Cornel West, *The War Against Parents: What We Can Do for America's Beleaguered Moms and Dads*. New York: Houghton Mifflin, 1998.

Hillman, James. *Healing Fiction*. Barrytown , N.Y.: Station Hill, 1983.

Hollies, Linda H. *Inner Healing for Broken Vessels: Seven Steps to Mending Childhood Wounds*. New York: Welstar Publications, 1990.

Hopewell, James. *Congregations, Stories, and Structures*. Philadelphia: Fortress Press, 1987.

Hunter, Rodney. "The Bible in Pastoral Practice: Themes and Challenges." In *Practical Theology and Pastoral Care: The Bible as Pastor*, 4-7. Cardiff, Wales: Cardiff University Press, 2006.

Hurst, David. "The Shepherding of Black Christians." Th.D. Dissertation. School of Theology at Claremont, 1981.

Jewett, Robert. *Romans: A Commentary*. Minneapolis: Fortress Press, 2007.

Kaufman, Gershen. *The Psychology of Shame: Theory and Treatment of Shame Based Syndromes*. New York: Springer, 1989.

Kynes, Bernard J. "Race and Personhood." In *The Journal of The Interdenominational Theological Center* (Spring 1998): 152-69.

Lankton, Carol H., and Stephen R. Lankton. *Tales of Enchantment: Goal-oriented Metaphors for Adults and Children in Therapy*. New York: Brunner & Mazel, 1989.

Lartey, Emmanuel Y. *In Living Colour: An Intercultural Approach to Pastoral Care and Counseling*. London: Cassell, 1997.

Lattimore, Vergel L. "The Positive Contribution of Black Values to Pastoral Counseling." In *Journal of Pastoral Care* 34 (June 1982): 105-17.

Lindemann, Erich. "Symptomatology and Management of Acute Grief." In

Crisis Intervention, edited by Howard J. Parad. New York: Family Service Association, 1976.

McCrary, Carolyn L. "Pastoral Care Strategies of Black Pastors." Ph.D. Dissertation. Northwestern University, 1984.

————. "The Wholeness of Women." In *The Journal of The Interdenominational Theological Center* (Spring 1998): 258-394.

McCrary, Carolyn L., and Edward P. Wimberly. "Personhood in African-American Pastoral Care." In *The Journal of The Interdenominational Theological Center* (Spring 1998): 5-7.

Mincy, Ronald B. *Black Males Left Behind.* Washington, D.C.: Urban Institute Press, 2006.

Mitchell, Henry, and Nicholas C. Lewter. *Soul Theology.* San Francisco: Harper & Row, 1986.

Oglesby, E. Hammon. *Pressing Toward the Mark: Christian Ethics for the Black Church Today.* Eugene, Oreg.: Wipf and Stock, 2007.

Parkes, Murray C. "Seeking and Finding a Lost Object: Evidence from Recent Studies of the Reaction to Bereavement." In *Social Science and Medicine* 4 (1970): 187-201.

Patton, John. *Is Human Forgiveness Possible?* Nashville: Abingdon Press, 1985.

Penner, Mary. *My Kids Are Hurting: A Survival Guide to Working with Students in Pain.* Grand Rapids: Zondervan, 2005.

Rasmus, Rudy. *Touch: The Power of Touch in Transforming Lives.* Friendswood, Tex. and Houston, Tex.: Baxter Press and Spirit Rising, 2006.

Rivers, Clarence J. "The Oral African Tradition Versus the Ocular Tradition." In *This Far by Faith: American Black Culture and Its African Roots.* Washington, D.C.: The National Office of Black Catholics, 1977.

Schnarch, David M. *Constructing the Sexual Crucible: An Integration of Sexual and Marital Therapy.* New York: W. W. Norton, 1991.

Smith, Archie, Jr. *Navigating the Deep River: Spirituality in African American Families.* Cleveland: United Church Press, 1997.

————. *The Relational Self Ethics and Therapy from a Black Church Perspective.* Nashville: Abingdon Press, 1982.

Smith, Archie, and Ursula Riedel-Pfaefflin. *Siblings by Choice: Race, Gender, and Violence.* St. Louis: Chalice Press, 2004.

Snorton, Teresa E. "The Legacy of the African-American Matriarch: New Perspectives for Pastoral Care." In *Through the Eyes of Women,* edited by Jeanne Stevenson-Moessner, 50-65. Minneapolis: Fortress Press, 1996.

_____. "Self Care for African American Women." In *In Her Own Way*, edited by Jeanne Stevenson-Moessner, 285-94. Minneapolis: Fortress Press, 2000.

Washton, Arnold M. *Cocaine Addiction: Treatment, Recovery and Relapse Prevention*. New York: W. W. Norton, 1989.

Wells, April C. "The Church's Contribution to Patriarchy: Destruction of Mental, Emotional, Spiritual Health of Women." In *The Journal of The Interdenominational Theological Center*. Spring 1998, 110-38.

West, Cornel. *Race Matters*. New York: Vintage Books, 1993.

White, Michael. *Narratives of Therapists' Lives*. Adelaide, South Australia: Dulwich Centre Publications, 1997.

White, Richelle. *Daughters of Imani: A Christian Rites of Passage Program for African American Young Women*. Nashville: Abingdon Press, 2005.

Wiley, Christine Y. "The Impact of a Parish-Based Pastoral Counseling Center on Counselors and Congregation: A Womanist Perspective." D.Min. dissertation, Garrett-Evangelical Theological Seminary, Evanston, Ill., 1994.

Wimberly, Anne Streaty, and Edward P. Wimberly. *The Winds of Promise: Building and Maintaining Strong Clergy Families*. Nashville: Discipleship Resources, 2007.

Wimberly, Edward P. *African American Pastoral Care and Counseling: The Politics of Oppression and Empowerment*. Cleveland: Pilgrim Press, 2006.

_____. "The Bible as Pastor: An African American Perspective." In *Contact: Practical Theology and Pastoral Care: The Bible as Pastor*. Cardiff, Wales: Cardiff University Press, 2006.

_____. *Claiming God, Reclaiming Dignity: African American Pastoral Care*. Nashville: Abingdon Press, 2003.

_____. *A Conceptual Model for Pastoral Care*. Ann Arbor: University of Michigan Micro!lms, 1976.

_____. *Counseling African American Marriages and Families*. Louisville: Westminster John Knox, 1997.

_____. *Moving from Shame to Self-Worth: Preaching and Pastoral Counseling* (Nashville: Abingdon Press, 1999).

_____. *Pastoral Care in the Black Church*. Nashville: Abingdon Press, 1979.

_____. "Pastoral Care of Sexual Diversity in the Black Church." In *Pastoral Care and Counseling in Sexual Diversity*. New York: The Haworth Pastoral Press, 2001.

_____. *Pastoral Counseling and Spiritual Values*. Nashville: Abingdon Press, 1982.

_____. *Prayer in Pastoral Counseling*. Louisville: Westminster Press, 1990.

_____. "Race and Sex in the Debate over Homosexuality in The United Methodist Church." In *Staying the Course: Supporting the Church's Position on Homosexuality*. Nashville: Abingdon Press, 2003.

_____. *Recalling Our Own Stories: Spiritual Renewal for Religious Caregivers*. San Francisco: Jossey-Bass, 1997.

_____. *Relational Refugees: Alienation and Reincorporation in African American Churches and Communities*. Nashville: Abingdon Press, 2000.

_____. "Spiritual Formation in Theological Education and Psychological Assessment." In *Clergy Assessment and Career Development*, edited by Richard A. Hunt, John E. Hinkle, and H. Newton Malony. Nashville: Abingdon Press, 1990.

_____. *Using Scripture in Pastoral Counseling*. Nashville: Abingdon Press, 1994.

Wimberly, Edward P., and Anne E. Wimberly. *Liberation and Human Wholeness*. Nashville: Abingdon Press, 1986.

Wimberly, Edward P., Anne Streaty Wimberly, and Annie Grace Chingonzo. "Pastoral Counselling, Spirituality and the Recovery of the Village Functions: African and African-American Correlates in the Practice of Pastoral Care and Counselling." In *Spirituality and Culture in Pastoral Care and Counseling*, edited by John Fosket and Emmanuel Lartey. Cardiff, Wales: Cardiff Academic Press, 2004.

Wurmser, Leon. *The Mask of Shame*. Baltimore: Johns Hopkins University Press, 1981.